"As a late-diagnosed autistic adult, this workbook will be a useful tool t neurodiversity-affirming therapy. This workbook will assist late-diag accepting themselves and rewriting negative self-concepts they've formed from growing up in a neurotypical world. I particularly love the way that the workbook elements are sprinkled throughout the illuminating and accessible text that the author has clearly crafted as a love letter to late-diagnosed autistic people."

—**Kristen Hovet, MHS**, host of *The Other Autism* podcast

"All autistic adults must read this book, as well as parents with newly diagnosed children. Such information was controversial when my book was published in 2000, championing the right of young people to understand their diagnosis. I am thrilled with Penot's new book! It takes this important work further by helping the adult reader 'find a path to living without the mask,' as Penot eloquently writes, and provides a courageous and practical road map."

—**Catherine Faherty,** Social Stories Trainer; former TEACCH Advanced Consultant; Autism Society of NC Professional; and author of three books, including *Autism…What Does It Mean to Me?*

"A user-friendly and practical resource for those looking to gain a good understanding of the function masking serves in navigating their way through a neurotypical world, and how to 'take off the mask' to live a more authentic and fulfilling life. Highly recommended for autistic folks that are looking for a 'map' to guide them through this process."

—**Christopher J. Quarto, PhD**, professor of professional counseling at Middle Tennessee State University, and host of the *Adult Autism* podcast

"*The Unmasking Workbook for Autistic Adults* is an essential read. It offers a compassionate and insightful look at the challenges and joys of autistic life, with wonderful activities to help organize and manage one's thoughts and feelings. With a focus on promoting inclusion and self-empowerment, the book is the ultimate resource for anyone looking to make a positive difference in their lives."

—**Francis Tabone, PhD**, head of Cooke School and Institute, and author of *The ASD Independence Workbook* and *Autism Spectrum Disorder*

The Unmasking Workbook for Autistic Adults

Neurodiversity-Affirming Skills
to Help You Live Authentically,
Avoid Burnout & Thrive

Jessica Penot, LPC-S

New Harbinger Publications, Inc.

Publisher's Note

This publication is designed to provide accurate and authoritative information in regard to the subject matter covered. It is sold with the understanding that the publisher is not engaged in rendering psychological, financial, legal, or other professional services. If expert assistance or counseling is needed, the services of a competent professional should be sought.

Printed in the United States of America

26   25   24

10   9   8   7   6   5   4   3   2   1   First Printing

This book is dedicated to all the autistic adults in the Tree of Life Autistic Adult Support Group. You all have taught me more than you know and have helped me learn how deeply beautiful and brilliant autistic people can be.

Contents

Introduction

When I was four years old, I was sitting on the steps in our big blue house in Tiffan, Ohio, and watching my parents fight. In that moment, I thought I was lucky not to be a person like them because, to me, people made everything so much more difficult than it needed to be. Later, when I realized I was a person, I was brokenhearted. Being a person seemed terrible.

All my life, I have felt like I wasn't human. I never knew what I was, but I felt deeply that I wasn't human. I felt like I was an outsider pretending to be human. As I aged, this sense of "otherness" led to being picked on and bullied by peers. Adults always seemed horrified by my behavior, and I never understood why. I would try to figure out why everyone was always mad at me, but it didn't make sense. People would say things like I was being "difficult" or "disrespectful" and I didn't know what that meant. I knew what I was doing was wrong, but I failed to understand what would be right. I knew I ate wrong, but the thought of eating what adults wanted me to eat was on par with the thought of eating poop, so the dinner table in my house became a war zone.

At school, I was told by teachers and peers that I needed to learn to act right. I was called weird. I was ostracized and left alone, and I struggled to figure out what the normal girls did to gain acceptance. Eventually, I began to study the other children who people accepted more and mimic their behaviors. If you are autistic, you know that this is what we must do to gain acceptance. We must become chameleons. We must mask. "Masking" is when we suppress certain behaviors autistic people find soothing, but that others think are "weird," such as stimming or having intense interests. We attempt to camouflage autistic traits to make neurotypical (someone who is neurologically more like the general population) people more comfortable. Although females are usually better at this than those assigned male at birth, almost all autistic people do this. I fit the female norm perfectly in this regard. I am adept at masking and can seem almost normal in most social circumstances. However, as you likely experience too, the amount of work that goes into appearing normal is beyond exhausting.

If you're like me, while you can copy behavior, you may never understand what normal is. You may watch conversations and their complexities elude you. This can lead to crippling anxiety. For example, I didn't understand how normal people knew what to do with their face and hands in social settings. If I didn't know what to do with them, I would feel like I couldn't breathe. When you are with people, the anxiety may be constant and overwhelming because it is fueled by messages you are always receiving. People may tell you that you talk too much, talk too fast, dress weird, smell weird, move too much, say the wrong thing at the wrong time, don't respond properly to emotional situations, don't listen, fidget…the list goes on. The more you hear these things, the more you feel you are wrong.

Over the years, your parents likely struggled to show you and teach you what normal was. But you may not understand why anyone would want to participate in most normal social interactions. They often seem pointless and boring. The rituals seem arbitrary, so even when you manage to mimic them, it feels tedious and horrible. This can lead to unbearable anxiety. For me, I knew interactions would eventually go wrong, leading to embarrassment and people abandoning me.

The Relief of Being Diagnosed

Like many females and people assigned female at birth who are autistic, I wasn't diagnosed as autistic until I was an adult, at forty-two years old. Like many people diagnosed in adulthood, I self-diagnosed and took tests online before I was able to be officially diagnosed by a professional. In the book *Women and Girls with Autism Spectrum Disorder* (2015), Sarah Hendrickx explains most women aren't diagnosed as autistic until later in life due to their proficiency in masking. Although late diagnosis is more common in women, numerous men also aren't diagnosed until later in life because of their masking skills.

When I finally got my diagnosis, it was nothing short of miraculous. I have spent my entire life hating myself for all the things I couldn't do. Like me, you may have spent a lifetime berating yourself for not being able to learn skills that seem basic. So when you got an official diagnosis, it may have felt like you could breathe for the first time. You can finally give yourself grace. You can forgive yourself for the mountain of "mistakes" that lie behind you and move forward on a new path.

In the show *Douglas*, Hannah Gadsby describes getting her diagnosis as autistic as "finding the keys to the kingdom of myself." This is what it feels like being diagnosed as an adult. You have likely spent much of your life trying desperately to hide yourself from everyone. When you feel fundamentally flawed and bizarre on a level that could never be loved or understood, you feel like an alien masquerading as a human. Autism can give a name to what you are and provide a road map for you to begin to find happiness. It won't be happiness like neurotypicals know it, but it will be happiness.

Even after your diagnosis frees you, you'll likely still struggle with the trauma of growing up in a world that never accepted you. Here's how this trauma affects me: I apologize for almost everything. I am quick to assume that any mistake in an interpersonal interaction must be my fault. I have been in unhealthy and toxic relationships because I don't understand boundaries and I was raised to believe that I am so difficult that everything wrong in any human interaction must be my fault. I am prone to constant anxiety after any human interaction and overanalyze it, trying to find all the errors I may have made because as I was told that all of my behavior was bad as a child, I assume that I have made a million mistakes. Does any of that sound familiar in your experience?

The True Struggle We Face

In the autistic community, there sometimes seems to be discord between the perspectives of autistic adults as expressed on social media, YouTube, in therapy, and in blogs and the professional community. The general feeling expressed by most autistic adults is that the professional community tends to lean on old childhood models of treatment without listening to autistic adults who have lived these experiences. Recently, more and more autistic adults—such as me—are going into the field of psychology, so there has been a solid push to integrate autistic voices into treatment needs to reflect our experiences while also being driven by research.

I have been working with autistic people as a therapist for seven years now. As I listen to their stories, I know their struggles as intimately as I know my own struggles. We feel isolated and alone, going through life without many reliable friends or social connections because we also are autistic. All our energy is spent trying to hide stimming and trying to talk like normal people talk. We are rejected by normal people despite our best efforts and never really understand why we were rejected.

I also know the answer can't be for us just to learn normal social skills. Too many crisis calls with too many clients arise when we try to use those social skills and still fail. Like my clients, you may cry and say, "Why can't I just be normal?" I have lived this and watched this for too long. I know the answer can never be for us to learn to act like "normal" people because we simply aren't normal people. This "acting normal" is called *masking*, the immense effort that many autistic adults have to make every day to appear normal, which takes a toll on our well-being.

It is even more ironic that social skills, behavior modification, and camouflaging autistic traits remain the focus of autism treatments because these aren't the primary concerns of most autistic people. The concerns I hear most frequently include:

- Anxiety

- Depression

- Self-esteem issues

- Not being able to understand and interpret other people's emotions (alexithymia)

- Executive function issues

- Meltdowns and shutdowns

- Difficulties communicating with and being understood by others

- Being too easily overwhelmed and stressed by sensory issues

- Being too easily overwhelmed by daily life stressors

- Constant fear of doing something wrong or upsetting someone

- Constant people-pleasing or going above and beyond to prevent people from being mad you

- Searching for activities that bring happiness

- Finding ways to understand and be understood by others (dual empathy)

- Difficulty understanding your own emotions and the emotions of others

- Difficulty setting and understanding boundaries

- Knowing who you are underneath all the masking you have been forced to do

- Difficulties with all types of relationships (friendships, pair bonded relationships, and family)

- Trauma (from bullying, toxic relationships, etc.)

These aren't all the issues autistic people have. Our issues are as diverse as the face of autism itself, but no matter how you look at it, most treatments for autism that are commonly available don't look at the real-life needs and desires of autistic adults.

Autistic people live lives most neurotypicals will never understand. We are born different and there isn't anything we can do about it. Our lives are shaped by childhoods riddled with constant criticism, irritation, and alienation by almost every other human being that we encounter. We know we are different, and we also know we can't be like normal people.

Autistic adults and adolescents share a similar sense of angst regarding normative social interactions. Small talk is generally considered aversive, and standard to-and-fro conversation is weird and awkward. Many of us don't know what to do with our faces. We crave a different kind of social interaction. We crave different answers to the ones we have been given. In the book *NeuroTribes* (2015), author Steve Silberman says that we don't need to have our difficulties eliminated, but instead learn to cope with special challenges using special strategies. We don't need to be aware that we are different, but that we are responsible for our lives. In other words, we are not broken. We just need new ways of being in control of our lives that aren't based on neurotypical models.

The goal of this book is to create a new way of treating autism that focuses on unmasking, being genuine, and relearning who you are as an autistic adult. I aim to integrate the concerns I have heard working with autistic adults with concerns the online autistic community has expressed to me regarding the current research about quality of life for autistic adults. We can create a new way of coping with and treating autism that doesn't focus on taking the autism away. Rather, it can focus on making the unique stressors that come from being autistic easier to bear—stressors that come both from the disability itself and from living in an ableist, neurotypical world.

You don't have to mask, hide, or camouflage. Until you learn to love yourself, you will always be doomed to live in the shadows of the neurotypical world. This book can help you discover self-compassion by looking at yourself as you are, not as the world has taught you that you should be. You can discover the beauty of yourself as an autistic human. Let's begin this journey of self-discovery and acceptance.

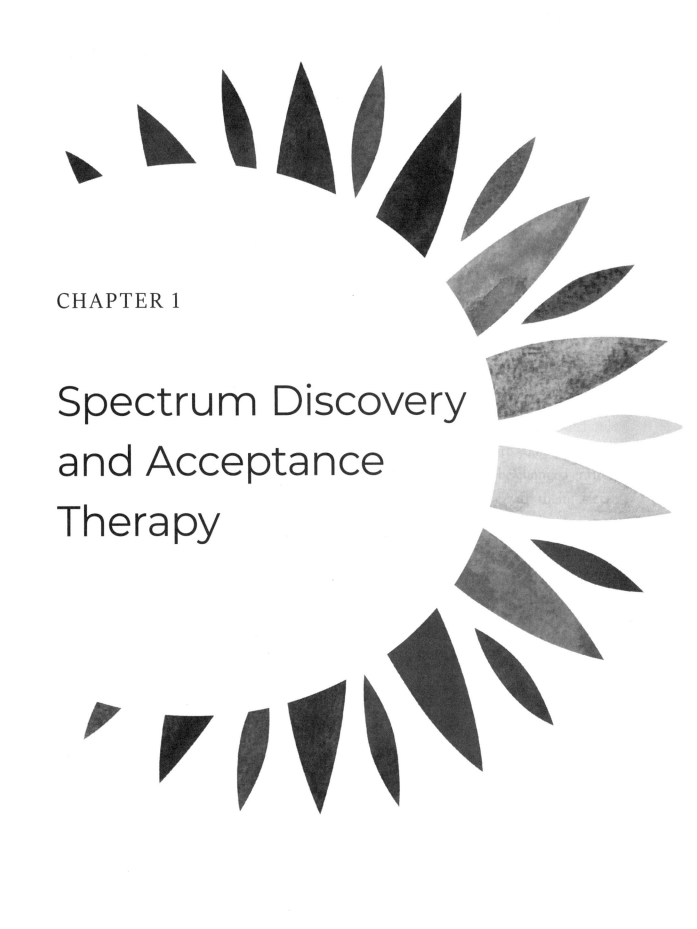

CHAPTER 1

Spectrum Discovery and Acceptance Therapy

The neurotypical worlds of self-help, philosophy, art, and parenting are littered with a recurring message: *happiness comes from learning to be yourself.* This message is loud, and it is everywhere. Google self-love and hundreds of these messages emerge:

- Taylor Swift said, "Just be yourself, there is no one better."

- Lady Gaga said, "Do not allow people to dim your shine because they are blinded. Tell them to put on some sunglasses, 'cuz we were born this way, bitch!"

- Roy Bennett said, "You were born to stand out, stop trying to fit in."

- Lao Tzu said, "The snow goose need not bathe to make itself white. Neither need you do anything but be yourself."

- J. A. Redmerski said, "Just remember to always be yourself and don't be afraid to speak your mind and dream out loud."

"Love yourself exactly as you are" is the message for neurotypicals and their children. Advice that is commonly given to neurotypicals during new social engagements is "just be yourself." If you are going someplace new you should "just be yourself." If you are going on a date, you should "just be yourself." This advice is peppered with other messages, like "trust your gut" and "use common sense." These are the messages of self-love that neurotypical children are raised with. If you are yourself, the right people will love you for who you are. Even deeper than that the message is that you have something within you that, if you trust it, things will work out.

However, those of us who have been autistic since childhood know that we have never received messages that sound anything like this. Most of us were given very different messages as children and many children today are still given those messages. The messages you were given as a child most likely linger in your mind and haunt you, convincing you that you need to second-guess everything you do. The messages that are given to autistic children are brutal:

- Autistic children are told to "use social narratives and social cartooning as tools in describing and defining social rules and expectations."

- The worst part of the messages given to us as children is that we weren't even allowed to receive these messages directly because we were considered too weird, broken, and incompetent to receive them. So our schools and caretakers were taught how to train us properly. Our caregivers were told to "teach imitation, motor as well as verbal" (Autism Speaks, School Community Tool Kit).

- Another example of messages sent to autistic people is from the social skills intervention by Connie Anderson: "One logical approach to treatment might be to break down social skills into their components and then teach these basic skills in a stepwise fashion" (Foden and Anderson 2011).

In other words, autistic children are taught to *learn to mimic normal people because they are fundamentally flawed.* You likely still feel these messages in your bones. These messages all say that, if you are yourself, no one will love you for who you are. They say that you don't know yourself and you must be taught how to be a proper person because if you act like you want to, you will be rejected. These messages keep you masking even when you know that masking hurts you and prevents you from finding the self-compassion you so desperately need. Unlearning these messages is one of the most important parts of finding contentment and increasing your quality of life.

What messages did you receive as a child? Were you told to love yourself for who you were or were you taught to hide your autistic traits? How did this impact you?

_____

_____

_____

_____

How ASD Has Been Perceived Through the Decades

The messages autistic children are taught have their roots in a long history of diagnosis and treatment, and you may find it helpful to know how these perceptions have changed through the decades. In 1943, Dr. Leo Kanner defined autism spectrum disorder (ASD) based on studying a group of young boys who had previously been thought to have mental retardation.

These boys had difficulty with speech and social interactions and engaged in ritualized and repetitive behaviors (Harris 2018). They didn't like transitions and any change in schedule or routine could lead to meltdowns. At the time, autism research was based on the most extreme cases. Most of the children studied had been placed in institutions and all were male. Research into this sample of autistic children progressed steadily and theories pervaded the profession quickly. The first theory was that poor parenting led to ASD. In 1967, Bruno Bettelheim noted that professionals blamed poor mothering and coined the term "refrigerator mother" to describe the parenting style that led to autism (Broderick 2022).

Over the last sixty years, the way professionals look at autism has changed greatly. However, it is still widely misunderstood. Pop culture depictions of autism and cultural phenomena, like the great vaccination autism scare, have led to perceptions of autism that are not only inaccurate, but even worse, depict autism as a disease that needs to be cured. The professional world hasn't done much to change this. Sarah Hendrickx's research (2015) shows that biases in the samples used to study autism led to the belief that females were almost never autistic. But females were rarely tested for autism until adulthood. This has changed and there has been a huge surge in females being tested in recent years, but the biases have yet to catch up with the data. These biases have also led to stereotyped assumptions about autistic people. When I was in graduate school in clinical psychology, we learned almost nothing about autism. What we did learn was based on the male model that assumed all autistic people were vaguely nonverbal males who liked trains and math.

Only in the past ten years has research emerged about the quality of life for autistic adults. Researchers and advocates have also worked to change the way people perceive and relate to autism. According to Steve Silberman (2015), "One of the most promising developments… has been the emergence of the concept of neurodiversity: the notion that conditions like autism, dyslexia, and ADHD should be regarded as naturally occurring cognitive variations with distinctive strengths that have contributed to the evolution of technology and culture rather than a mere checklist of deficits and dysfunctions." And as Barry Prizant writes in *Uniquely Human*, "Instead of trying to change how an autistic person reacts to us, we need to pay close attention to how we react to them." This implies that autistic people don't need to change things we are happy to have; rather, we need to accept that others may react to us poorly.

An explosion of new research has also changed the way professionals understand the disorder. Studies have shown that the correlation between autism and various genes indicates that ASD is more than likely caused by neurological differences rather than poor parenting, improper behavioral training, or vaccination history. One prevalent theory by Warrier and Cohen (2017) is that glial, synaptic, and chromatin pathway differences in the brain are a major contributing factor to the autism phenotype. Another interesting study by Keowon (2013) showed that "growing evidence indicates atypical long-distance connectivity in autism spectrum disorder." This suggests that those who are autistic have increased connections between neurons in certain regions of our brains.

One of the most fascinating areas of autism research is a theoretical construct called *monotropism*. This phrase was coined based on research done by Murray, Lawson, and Lesser (2019). Research into this concept began in 1992 and has produced some interesting theoretical approaches and explanations into the neurology of autism and the ways in which our brains are functionally very different. According to Murray et al. (2019), "Attention tunneling, hyper/hypo responses, intense interests, passionate minds, and splinter skills localize and concentrate to the exclusion of other input; an atypicality from which many other differences can be seen to follow." The research goes on to explain this unique feature of autism in terms of a "biologically grounded value system," which eloquently explains autism based on biology. The years of research that have followed this theory support the truth that autism is something hardwired, immutable, and unchangeable. There is no way for us to make ourselves normal. If the montopism construct is correct, our way of thinking and relating to the world is so different from normal that even mimicking normalcy effectively isn't possible. Thus, autism is not a disease; instead, those of us who are autistic are neurologically different. This atypical brain functioning leads us to relate to the world in a unique way.

Recent research also shows that the prevalence of autism is much higher than previously thought. According to the *Diagnostic and Statistical Manual of Mental Disorders* from 2013, one out of a hundred people were thought to be autistic. Today, the Centers for Disease Control's website indicates that more recent research puts prevalence rates closer to one in forty-four. Rates are significantly higher in females than previously thought (American Psychiatric Association 2022), but this explosion of research has yet to fully disseminate into popular culture and the work of everyday mental health professionals. Most of my clients who have been diagnosed as autistic using valid testing instruments come to me regularly with complaints of psychiatrists and doctors telling them they can't be autistic because "they don't seem autistic to them." Friends and family regularly question their diagnoses as well, leading to further emotional damage and hardship.

How ASD Has Been Treated Through the Decades

The primary treatment focus for autism has historically assumed that autistic people would be happier if they could learn social skills and act more normal. Most treatments were designed to help the parents of autistic children who have sought to integrate their children into normal society. Almost all regular treatments for autism are driven by principles that were derived from applied behavioral analysis (ABA). This treatment modality uses principles from behavioralism to teach autistic children how to integrate into neurotypical society. This treatment model was founded in the 1960s and positive outcomes were determined by behavioral measures. ABA has been improved to represent the concerns of autism advocates since the 1960s, but it remains the primary treatment modality for autism.

Although ABA has been helpful for parents of autistic children, there is still no consensus on a treatment that helps improve the quality of life for autistic adults. Current treatment modalities focus very much on autistic children. They also focus primarily on changing the behaviors of autistic people, and this doesn't help with the internal struggles adults and adolescents have. According to Moss, Mandy, and Howlin (2017):

> "In the decades since autism was first formally described in the 1940s, there have been major advances in research relating to diagnosis, causation, and treatment approaches for autistic children. However, research into prognosis, outcomes, or effective interventions for autistic adults is much more limited. The findings indicate that, as adults, many people who are autistic, including those of normal IQ, are significantly disadvantaged regarding employment, social relationships, physical and mental health, and quality of life. Support to facilitate integration within the wider society is frequently lacking, and there has been almost no research into ways of developing more effective intervention programs for adults. Moreover, most of the research on outcome has involved relatively young people in their 20s and 30s—much less is known about outcomes for autistic people as they reach mid-late adulthood."

Autistic adults are often forgotten and the messages we are left with don't allow for self-love and grace in the sometimes rigid mind of an autistic adult. Another conundrum is that many ways therapists and professionals relate to autism focuses on well-meaning attempts to get us to act more normal. Many of my clients have spent significant time with professionals who attempted to help them meet neurotypical social expectations so they would be better liked. This seems intuitively useful, because people might be happier if they could make friends more easily and blend in better. However, that is not always the case. I met with a psychiatrist who referred one of my clients to social skills training and when I argued with her, she said, "How can you expect this person to be happy if they don't have friends? Do you know what it is like to go through life without friends? They need to learn to be like normal people." This is a standard response of many neurotypical clinicians, and it can lead to the following problems:

- According to a study published in 2021 by Galvin, Howes, McCarthy, and Richards, there is direct link between lack of self-compassion and depression in autistic people. Autistic people who view themselves as weird and push themselves to be normal suffer 41.9 percent higher rates of depression than those who learn to love themselves as they are and grant themselves self-compassion and understanding.

- According to a study done by Alicia Broderick (2022), masking is the largest cause of emotional distress in autistic people. She found that the very act of trying to be normal and fake social skills causes significant depression and anxiety in autistic people.

- In another study it was found that 72 percent of autistic adults score above the average suicidality rate (Cassidy et al. 2018). This is because depression, anxiety, and isolation plague autistic adults and lead to increased rates of suicidality. It was also found that by decreasing masking, many of these symptoms could be alleviated.

Ironically, most treatments for autism have historically focused on teaching people the very skills that lead to decreased life expectancy and increased suicidality. Social skills training and other regularly used treatments heavily rely on a philosophy that pushes autistic people to learn to act like neurotypicals. Sadly, in most places, if you are autistic, these are still the treatments that are available to you (at least until you picked up this book).

Have you received any treatments for your autism? What were they? Did they help?

_____

_____

_____

_____

_____

_____

Self-Acceptance Is Essential for Us, Too

We must realize the messages we have been given are toxic. Very few people would consider creating any kind of manual for giving neurotypicals these messages. Very few people would consider teaching neurotypical children, "Everything you do and say is wrong. People will hate and bully you for who you are and how you act because it is irritating and to prevent this you must learn to copy the behaviors of others." Yet this is considered a perfectly normal thing to say to an autistic child or adult. I find it particularly strange that therapists, artists, philosophers, and ancient sages from almost every culture all know that happiness comes through self-acceptance and love, but that no one ever thought that these same rules might apply to autistic people.

This is the crux of the issue as we begin to look at how to find a balanced life with ASD. Those of us who are autistic are weird. We are different. We may be irritating to normative society, but that doesn't mean we deserve any less. We deserve to find beauty in ourselves and learn unique coping strategies for our stressors. This begins first with relearning who we are because most of us have been taught to hide our true selves. We have been taught through years of emotional abuse, nagging, and ostracization by schools, peers, parents, siblings, and almost every human we meet that who we are is wrong. Because of this, we learn to hide and be ashamed of ourselves.

Have you been abused, nagged, ostracized, or bullied due to your autistic traits? How?

_____

_____

_____

_____

_____

_____

_____

The first step to healing is to unlearn these negative messages. You have nothing to be ashamed of. You are beautiful. Even if neurotypicals around you don't tell you this, you deserve love and respect for exactly who you are at your core. Even if you stim and bounce and spin and repeat the same two words over and over. Even if you can't go to public places because they are too loud. Even if you have been working hard to hide your true self and appear normal to most people. Even if you want to talk about cars or signs or bugs or history until the neurotypicals back out of the room, you are wonderful and there are people who will love you for who you are. Learning to find yourself and love yourself is the beginning of the path to breaking the depression and anxiety that are the constant bedfellows of autistic people.

Fortunately, the perception of autism is beginning to change for the next generations, as children's books explore this topic. One of my favorite children's books is *Stellaluna* (Cannon 2007). In this beautifully illustrated story, a small fruit bat falls into a bird's nest after her mother is attacked by an owl. The mother bird lovingly tries to raise the small fruit bat, but no matter how hard the bat tries, it can't please the mother bird and is mocked by the other baby birds. She does everything wrong. She won't eat the right food. She won't perch correctly. She wants to be awake and sleep at the wrong times. The bat is humiliated and miserable. It isn't until the bat gets lost flying and discovers her true nature that she is free to be happy.

Yet, even discovering that she is a fruit bat isn't enough. She must unlearn all the hurt from being raised to be a bird. She has to relearn how to be a bat. Finally, she goes back to the birds and shows them that she is a bat and has learned to love herself as a bat. This is very similar to the unmasking process that autistic people need. It isn't enough to learn we are bats that have been raised by birds; we must also relearn how to live as bats and love ourselves as bats.

Discovering your true self is only the first part of this journey. Because most of us have been taught to hide all our intrinsic traits, even after we relearn and accept who we are, we must figure out how to cope with the things that make us different. If the first phase of unmasking is discovering who you really are, then the second stage of unmasking is accepting it, coping with it, embracing it, and loving yourself as a bat.

The Path to Learning to Be Yourself

I think the most beautiful moments of my adult life are the moments when I choose to love myself for the bat I am. There are people who don't like me. There are failed friendships and relationships, but there are also profound moments of connection over my hyperfixations. There are moments when I realize I am in public stimming with my service dog at my side, and even though some people avoid me, others find me and tell me about their autistic children and friends. I am able to have real, human connections for the first time in my life. It allows me to tell people that if they talk to me too much, I get overwhelmed. When I set boundaries, I can keep my quiet time and space sacred. Accepting myself allows me to same food ("same fooding" is the act of eating the same food for most meals most days) without shame. With grace, I can shut down for a few days without being riddled with self-loathing. Even my parents accept me for the first time in my life, and understanding autism has given them a template to connect with me.

Life is better here. It is better now that I can finally, finally just be me. There are people in my life who have helped me discover *dual empathy*, a place where they empathize with me and see my unique perspective and I can try to see theirs. I have also found immense connection and understanding by befriending other autistic adults. These are examples of what might be possible for you also, as you discover the bat you are.

In what ways have you begun loving yourself for your differences? What do you love about yourself?

_____

_____

_____

_____

_____

Disconnects Between Neurotypical Expectation and Autism's Reality

The path to learning to be yourself is a long and complex one and there are many unique obstacles for you to overcome that neurotypicals will never have to face. For example, one of the largest struggles most of my clients have is coping with *alexithymia*—the inability to recognize or describe our own emotions. You may struggle to understand what you are feeling, both emotionally and physically. This can lead to trying to reason your way through life's problems, and you may get lost in the knots of your own logic and become paralyzed. You likely don't know how to have the "gut" reactions so many neurotypicals rely upon.

You have emotions. They are there, and they are overwhelming, but you struggle to label and understand them the way neurotypicals have taught you. The result is that you can't come up with ways to easily deal with them. So even after you pull the mask away, you need to learn to cope with things like alexithymia that the neurotypical world has failed to provide an instruction manual for how to deal with. I want this book to be your instruction manual.

Another example of the disconnect between neurotypical expectations and our autistic reality is meltdowns and shutdowns. Because of the overconnectivity in certain regions of your brain, you are more easily overwhelmed by sensory and emotional input than neurotypicals. Your peripheral autonomic nervous system doesn't function like neurotypicals', so your fight-or-flight responses are not like theirs, so you might melt down or shut down. For me, meltdowns and shutdowns are the most embarrassing parts of my autism. I am a grown woman who still has to go sit in the closet when I have had too much stimuli. I have unmasked and I love myself for who I am, but whenever I have to work sixty hours a week and go to social events I become overwhelmed and have a meltdown.

My deepest struggles are things that neurotypical professionals have no template for. When I try to describe my experiences as an autistic adult, they look at me like I am teetering on a psychotic break. They say things like, "You didn't really sit in the closet?" Or "You might need medication for that." The truth is, I feel fine most days. But neurotypical professionals still treat me like I am broken and lost because I cope with the world in ways they don't find acceptable. It doesn't matter that I say I am content if I need a dog and time in my closet—to them, I am seriously mentally ill and need medication. My behavior will always be odd and many neurotypicals can't accept that. But I can accept it and love myself and that is what matters. Neurotypicals, even neurotypical professionals, may never understand or validate you. Accept that your disability is valid, your way of relating to the world can be healthy, and you are perfect just the way you are...or at least as perfect as anyone can be.

You may battle with the process of unmasking and self-discovery in a way that feels horrifying. I want you to know what it's like at the end of that journey. I have discovered ways to find beauty in my hyperfixations. I don't care what neurotypicals think of me. I have a few close friends who are also neurodivergent or are quirky in their own ways. I have a service dog that helps me cope with feelings of overwhelm that I get in public places. I am happy being a fruit bat and I have no desire to be a bird.

The following quote is often attributed to Albert Einstein. While he didn't say this, the quote is beautiful: "Everyone is a genius. But if you judge a fish by its ability to climb a tree it will live its whole life believing that it is stupid." The goal of this workbook is to teach you to be the beautiful person you are—because fish will never be able to climb trees. Swimming is just as magical as climbing a tree. So be a fish in your own pool of water.

CHAPTER 2

Excavating Yourself

We begin life in a bubble and our brains are designed to adapt to our bubble. Most people are born into a specific culture with neurologically similar people and their brains are designed to conform to *those* people and *that* environment. This is very functional and very adaptive on many levels. We learn to survive in our environments, and for neurotypicals this is usually a streamlined process.

Neurotypicals are born to a family that is neurologically similar and they can learn and adapt to their environments similarly. According to research by Stephen Porges (2017), one of the first functions of young humans is an autonomic nervous system–based function. Our fight, flight, and safety systems attune to our environment, and we learn that our parents are safe. We can then model behaviors after them, and learn and grow up in a world where we form safe attachments to other humans. Then we engage in this world in a way that is normal for the society we are raised in.

However, the first thing you need to accept as an autistic person is that *you were not neurologically capable of any of this.* This isn't your fault. You didn't do anything wrong. You are different. Your brain is different than that of neurotypicals. A multitude of studies show this. For example, research by van Rooij et al. (2018) shows that autistic people have a thinner temporal cortex (a region associated with speech and auditory processing), a thicker frontal cortex (a region associated with complex cognitive processes), and a smaller amygdala (the emotional hub of the brain).

Negative Messages

You are not like neurotypicals. Expecting yourself to be able to function and adapt like a neurotypical is a recipe for unending anxiety and depression. You can't expect a fish to fly. You couldn't adapt to your environment like other children could, and this inability to adapt like a neurotypical child probably led to you being bullied, ostracized, isolated, singled out in school, yelled at by parents and caregivers, and in some circumstances abused. It probably led to a sense of profound otherness and a feeling that you didn't belong, even in your family.

The first step is to acknowledge that all of this was wrong. You didn't deserve any of this. You are different. You are odd. You aren't like other people.

You are wonderful just the way you are!

I can say this, but for most of us it is hard to believe. It is hard to believe because throughout our entire lives we have received messages that conflict with this.

Circle any of the following that you were told throughout your childhood:

- *I was difficult.*

- *I was too much.*

- *I was bad.*

- *I was too loud.*

- *I talked too much.*

- *I was selfish.*

- *I didn't care about other people.*

- *I fidgeted too much.*

- *I walked like a truck driver.*

- *People wouldn't like me.*

- Other: _____

  _____

Circle any of the following that you experienced throughout your childhood:

- *I was yelled at.*

- *I was criticized.*

- *I was often punished.*

- *I was punished in school.*

- *I was punished by my parents.*

- *I was isolated by peers.*

- *I was bullied.*

- Other: _____

  _____

If you circled several of these messages and experiences, it may feel difficult to unmask. The first step has to be believing that it is okay to unmask. You can unlearn these messages and accept that the people who said them were wrong. This doesn't mean you need to call them bad or stupid. It means that you accept that they didn't understand how to raise or help a neurodivergent child. They were birds trying to teach bats how to fly and they just didn't know how. They damaged you with messages they didn't fully understand themselves (if you were more purposefully abused, those messages need to be unlearned as well). So, this is where you have to begin. You must take stock of the messages to unlearn them, which you'll do in the following exercise. This exercise is also available online at http://www.newharbin ger.com/53509.

TAKE STOCK OF NEGATIVE MESSAGES

In the following chart, record the negative messages you received about your autistic self. Then write about how neurotypicals enforced this message. After you have gained this clarity, come up with new, positive messages about yourself that can counter the negative ones.

Negative Message About My Autistic Self	How It Was Reinforced	Positive Messages I Can Send Myself
Ex. If you keep fidgeting in public everyone will think you are a weirdo.	Parents and teachers nagged me about it. I was eventually put in timeout for stimming.	Stimming doesn't bother anyone. Lots of people use fidgets and stim. Stimming helps me calm down and reduces my anxiety, so it is good for me.
Ex. You talk too much and it is annoying. You are selfish and don't care about what other people have to say.	Teachers put notes in my report cards. I got silent lunch. Peers made fun of me. My mom put me in timeout and told me I was annoying and being difficult.	Info-dumping and talking about hyperfixated interests is one the best parts of autism. I am full of passion and I love being alive when I can be lost in something I am interested in and share it with the world.

Negative Message About My Autistic Self	How It Was Reinforced	Positive Messages I Can Send Myself

Respect Your Diagnosis

Some of the other negative messages sent to you might have to do with your autism diagnosis. This book assumes that you have been diagnosed as autistic, but it doesn't assume as to where or how. If you are reading this thinking, "I am pretty sure I am autistic, but I haven't been diagnosed," it is okay to take statistically valid and reliable online tests so you can validate your own self-diagnosis if you don't have the money or resources to get an official test by a psychologist. Online tests I recommend you take to validate your self-diagnosis are:

- Ritvo Autism Asperger Diagnostic Scale, Revised (RAADS-R)

- Camouflaging Autistic Traits Questionnaire (CAT-Q)

- Autism Spectrum Quotient (ASQ)

- Aspie Quiz

- Samantha Craft's Checklist for Women with Autism

While it is better to be tested by a qualified professional, many of the people I have spoken with can't always afford this. Plus, many of the testing facilities can be waitlisted more than a year out. It can be nearly impossible to get an official, clinical diagnosis.

Even if you have an official, clinical diagnosis, you may question it. You may have been told by doctors, medical professionals, family, and friends that they don't believe your diagnosis and they think you aren't autistic. This is because they don't understand autism, not necessarily because you aren't autistic. Using the tests above can help you validate yourself further. It can help remind you that in an invalidating world, you are an autistic adult. Your disability is real. You deserve help.

It is also okay if every clinician you visit doesn't agree with your diagnosis. Many professionals I have worked with like to say things like, "You don't seem autistic to me" or "This is just a TikTok fad." I don't judge them because much of the research into autism is new. Many professionals were trained ten or more years ago when autism was still viewed through the old perspectives that tended to spread the belief that all autistic people were boys who liked trains. Autism may not be their specialty. However, this should not impact your treatment. What matters most to your treatment is that you have been assessed and that your diagnosis helps you progress forward with a treatment program that helps your growth. Overall, many autistic people report being invalidated by health professionals at some point in their lives. It is important that you seek out perspectives from multiple sources before you write yourself off as "faking it," "using autism as a crutch," "lying," or "exaggerating."

Have you ever been invalidated by a mental health or medical professional? If so, how? How did this impact you?

_____

_____

_____

_____

_____

_____

People in your daily life might also invalidate your diagnosis, especially if it is late in life. It is important that you understand that all people have biases and are influenced by pop culture and messages sent by organizations like Autism Speaks. If you have been diagnosed as autistic and feel that this is who you are, letting others invalidate you can only contribute to anxiety and depression. Take the online tests listed above. Validate yourself. Talk to other autistic people. We are usually better at recognizing other autistic people than neurotypicals are.

Let Go of the Fear

Even as you increase your respect for your autism diagnosis, one of the largest obstacles you may face is fear of unmasking, letting go, and accepting your disability. Because of all the messages you listed before, it might feel terrifying and dangerous to show who you really are. You may fear invalidating messages. You may fear abandonment. You may fear anger and hostility. All of these are reasonable fears, but without facing these fears it will be difficult to move past the anxiety and depression that are the constant bedfellows of autism.

Have you been invalidated by people in your life or told that you are not likable when you act like yourself? How did this make you feel?

_____

_____

_____

_____

_____

_____

_____

Most of the people I work with struggle with loneliness. Although we enjoy quiet and are overwhelmed by people, most of us need safe, loving human contact just like all other human beings. This is often very difficult for us to obtain and maintain due to the social deficits intrinsic in autism. For us, the largest fears involved in unmasking are often that we will become more alone or we will remain alone forever. The goal of this book is to help you unmask and learn skills to avoid being alone. The following exercise will help you examine your fears around unmasking. This exercise is also available online at http://www.newharbin ger.com/53509.

EXAMINE YOUR FEAR OF UNMASKING

In the following chart, record your fears about unmasking and the strengths that will help you through the process.

What are you afraid will happen if you let go of the mask and allow yourself to be yourself?	What strengths do you have that you can use to face this fear? Are you smart? Are you good at losing yourself in hyperfixations? Do you have supportive family or friends? Are you happy being alone? Do you have special skills?
Ex. I am afraid that if I am my true self all my friends will abandon me and I will be alone.	People may leave me, but I enjoy being alone and I only need a few friends.
Ex. I am afraid that people will think I am a bad person and I will lose my job.	I am very good at my job and my ability to lose myself in my work makes me better at my job than most neurotypicals.

The Toll of Masking

The toll of masking is real and serious. Wiskerke, Stern, and Igelström (2018) studied the toll consistent masking or camouflaging behaviors took on autistic people. According to Wiskerke et al., "The adults interviewed described feeling utterly drained—mentally, physically, and emotionally. One woman, Mandy, explained that after camouflaging for any length of time, she needs to curl up in the fetal position to recover."

What do you do to help recover from long periods of masking?

_____

_____

_____

_____

Wiskerke et al. continue, "Others said they feel their friendships are not real because they are based on a lie, increasing their sense of loneliness. And many said they have played so many roles to disguise themselves through the years that they have lost sight of their true identity."

Because you don't feel you can be yourself in friendships, you may not feel close to people. Name the people you feel truly close to.

_____

_____

_____

_____

If you can't come up with many names, know that this is common—and so is the loneliness you may feel as a result.

Everyone changes their behaviors to fit in sometimes. Neurotypicals must hide certain traits in certain situations. The world requires adaptive behaviors designed to help people blend in with normative society. However, according to Russo (2018), "Camouflaging calls for constant and elaborate effort. It can help autistic women maintain their relationships and careers, but those gains often come at a heavy cost, including physical exhaustion and extreme anxiety."

When you mask or camouflage, what personality traits do you take on? Do you have different personalities for different situations?

_____

_____

_____

_____

_____

_____

This research is important because it shows across studies that masking leads to worse mental health. Masking is hurting you. The following exercise will help you analyze the damage that masking has done so you can begin to improve your quality of life and mental health. This exercise is also available online at http://www.newharbinger.com/53509.

EXPLORE THE DAMAGE OF MASKING

Take a moment to deeply evaluate the impact masking has had on your life. Think about the damage it has done and ask yourself if it was worth it. Use the following chart to document the ways you mask in your daily life. Write down why you do this and then examine how this causes you anxiety or distress.

How You Mask	Why You Mask	How Masking Has Created Distress
Ex. I hide my stimming by picking at my cuticles to keep my hands still.	I am very aware that people stare at me when I stim and flap my hands or fidget. This makes me feel weird and self-conscious and I imagine people are judging me.	I often pick my hands until they bleed to keep them still.
Ex. I make eye contact when I don't want to.	I was told that I had to make eye contact and if I didn't make eye contact I must not be listening or paying attention. I was punished at school and at home for seeming distracted and rude.	Eye contact is very uncomfortable to me. I feel naked and want to escape interactions because of the discomfort caused by this.

How You Mask	Why You Mask	How Masking Has Created Distress

The toll masking took on my life was enormous. I was terrible at masking in middle school and high school. I tried different masks, but they rarely worked and the friends I made were more than likely neurodivergent in one way or another. I put in a tremendous amount of work to change my behavior and personality so I could figure out what worked best to obtain and maintain friends, family relationships, and romantic partners. It wasn't until I was married and had children that I mastered the art of masking. Up until then, I was often shunned and told I was mean or rude. As a young mother, I learned that if I talked about my children and husband I was accepted into most female social circles. I learned to mimic the behaviors of the other women in the group, and I got very good at masking.

The rewards for learning to mask were magical to me. For the first time in my life, I was liked. Of course, I wasn't liked for myself, and it required a lot of effort to hide myself. Any slip of behavior into who I was led to massive anxiety. I also wasn't really as good at masking as I needed to be because I still often lost friends and many people found me odd and off-putting.

Despite the anxiety, I tried to hide everything about my autistic self that I could. There were even portions of my life where I masked so thoroughly and completely that when I went back and read my journals, I was narrating my private journal with my masked persona. Of course, over the years I lost myself and forgot who I was. I also became so depressed and anxious that I was living a life in which the only thing I genuinely looked forward to was sleep because it was the only place I could stop masking. I have found that this story is common for many autistic people. Is this story true for you?

Have you struggled with anxiety that your real self would come out? Describe the feeling.

_____

_____

_____

_____

What Is Behind the Mask?

Like me, you may not know who you are. You may feel you don't have the right to be yourself in a world that might find you annoying or aversive. But you do deserve to be who you are, and everyone is annoying and aversive to someone. There are people who will love you exactly as you are. You may have to find other autistic people, but you won't be alone.

So how do you rediscover who you are underneath all the years of social conditioning and masking and hiding and self-loathing? How do you find yourself? This is the goal of the next few exercises: to uncover who you were before the masking.

In your earliest memories, describe what you were like.

_____

_____

_____

_____

_____

If you stimmed, what did it feel like? How did you stim? When did you stim?

_____

_____

_____

Did you have strange interests? Describe them. Did they bring you positive or negative emotion?

_____

_____

_____

Did you talk a lot or not much at all? Describe what having a conversation felt like.

_____

_____

_____

What were your passions?

_____

_____

_____

What did you love about yourself?

_____

_____

_____

Next, it's important to examine your autistic traits and why you feel the need to hide them, which you'll do in the following exercise. This exercise is also available online at http://www.newharbinger.com/53509.

WHY YOU HIDE YOUR AUTISTIC TRAITS

Take a moment to think about your traits that are unique to autism. Many of us love our autistic traits but we hide them to make others happy. Describe the traits you love about your autistic self and if you hide them, think about why you hide them.

Autistic Traits or Quirks That Bring You Solace	Why You Hide Them
Ex. I love talking about my hyperfixated interests. Talking about things I love and engaging in intellectual pursuits that involve my passions makes me feel warm and happy.	People tell me I am selfish when I focus too much on one thing. I forget to do activities that I should be doing and don't notice other people's wants and needs. I talk too much. People are bored and irritated by me. I want to be liked and people say I am pretentious. I am afraid people won't like me if I don't hide this side of me.
Ex. I hate loud noises. They are painful to me. I can't focus and I feel the noise in my body. I want to leave whenever anything is too loud or tell people to be quiet.	I stay in situations that make me uncomfortable because people have told me I am selfish and self-centered when I react to loud noises. They say I don't care about things that make other people happy. I am afraid people will think I am weird or selfish if I ask for my needs to be met.

Autistic Traits or Quirks That Bring You Solace	Why You Hide Them

Now that you've looked at the reasons you hide, think about what you would do and how you would be if you didn't hide anymore. This is your place to dream big. the sky's the limit!

If all the opinions of others and the reasons you hide who you are were stripped away, how would you behave?

_____

_____

_____

_____

_____

What would you do with your hands? Would you move them? Would you doodle? Use a fidget toy?

_____

_____

_____

What would you do with your body? Would you bounce, pace, rock?

_____

_____

_____

What would you do with your face? Would you keep your face relaxed, or would you smile and laugh? Would you twitch your nose?

_____

_____

_____

What would your voice be like? Would it be quiet? Would you talk? Would you talk softly, loud, fast, or slow? Would you prefer to communicate in writing?

_____

_____

_____

What would you do when you are anxious? Would you cry? Hide in a closet? Hide under the covers? Yell? Laugh? Rock?

_____

_____

_____

How would you communicate? Would you repeat the same words or phrases? Would you speak softly or loudly? Would you info-dump about your favorite things?

_____

_____

_____

What would you do with your space? Would things be organized? Would you tell people not to touch your things? Would you sort things? Would things be messy?

_____

_____

_____

What would you do with your time? Would you follow a routine? What would the routine be? Would you work hard for a few months and then shut down? Would you work more or less on different things?

_____

_____

_____

What would you do with your people time? Would you be alone most of the time? Would you like one special person to parallel play (engage in different activities side by side) with? Would you like to interact mostly online?

_____

_____

_____

Embracing Your Atypical

In an article in the *Atlantic*, Olga Khazan (2020) writes, "People who are on the periphery of society tend to be freer to innovate and change social norms." She goes on to say that odd people are more successful and more creative. They are more likely to make changes in society that make a difference. She argues that people who adhere to social norms and mores may be more accepted, but they aren't the people who can change the world in unique and novel ways.

This can be seen in the impact autistic people make on society every day. The list of remarkable and unique autistic people who have made society better is long. It includes Anthony Hopkins, Albert Einstein, Henry Cavendish, Bobby Fischer, Emily Dickinson, Temple Grandin, Tim Burton, Hannah Gadsby, Bill Gates, Charles Darwin, Mark Zuckerberg, Sir Isaac Newton, Elon Musk, Nikola Tesla, James Taylor, Carl Jung, Daryl Hannah, and so many more. These are amazing people who found success in being different. In being strange. If Tim Burton didn't embrace everything that made him different from neurotypicals, we wouldn't have the beauty of his strange and surreal art. If Albert Einstein didn't embrace the fact that he was a "fish" and couldn't climb a tree, we wouldn't have the theory of relativity. Being normal and being neurotypical isn't the best or the only way to live.

I know that most of us will never be Albert Einstein. We won't be Emily Dickinson or Hannah Gadsby. We won't be famous, but this isn't the point. The point is that by letting go of the need to be like everyone else, these people were able to lose themselves in the parts of autism that make it beautiful. I may not make any groundbreaking discoveries in physics or make any remarkable movies, but I can tell you more about Clive Barker and the Hellraiser movies than any normal person can. That may make the neurotypicals flee in terror, but it will bring a few magical people closer to me and give me a chance to love and enjoy life on my own terms.

I am odd. I stand out as odd. I go into public places and people stare. I have a service dog that is with me all the time. I stim. I repeat my words. I info-dump. I do all these things, and I have had lonely years and I have known deep and bitter rejection, but I have also found a path to living without the mask. I have found a path to beauty in the strange corners of this world where there is peace and joy for those of us who don't quite belong.

CHAPTER 3

Find Your Place
on the Spectrum

Autism has been depicted in the media perhaps more than any other mental health concern. Sadly, its depiction has been problematic. In the 1990s, autism was viewed clinically and in the media as a condition that emerged with severe difficulties with social and communication skills in mostly male populations. The movie *Rain Man* depicted what was considered to be the normal profile for autism in the 1990s. This image was supported by the *DSM-3*, which maintained the description of autism as the most severe set of symptoms by separating what is now diagnostically autism into five different disorders. In the *DSM-4*, the pervasive developmental disorders (PDDs) included Asperger's syndrome, pervasive developmental disorder not otherwise specified (NOS), and autism spectrum disorder (ASD).

In the past, a diagnosis of PDD-NOS was given if a person was determined to have some traits of autism but didn't meet the full diagnostic criteria for conditions like autistic disorder and Asperger's syndrome. Asperger's syndrome is what would now be considered autism spectrum disorder level 1 or autism without the intellectual deficits that went hand in hand with autism by the *DSM-4* definition. The combining of three separate disorders into one disorder, ASD, has led to numerous problems with the way people understand and relate to autism in the media, popular culture, and individually. Autism is no longer just the image shown in *Rain Man*, but a huge spectrum that includes many phenotypical and behavioral variations and presentations.

Another massive event that shaped perceptions of autism was Wakefield et al.'s 1998 study in *The Lancet*. In this since-discredited study, Wakefield concluded that the measles, mumps, and rubella (MMR) vaccine caused autism. Despite the small sample size of this study (twelve) and the lack of a controlled scientific design, many very famous people got a hold of the study and started what is now known as the anti-vaccination movement. This study was refuted, and Andrew Wakefield admitted that he had falsified data, but that didn't stop the media storm that followed. The result was a depiction of autistic children to be worse or on par with a child who gets measles.

The worst symptoms and the most seriously impaired autistic people were put in the limelight and those who were more able to mask and hide their symptoms were forgotten. During this time, the massive organization Autism Speaks gained a foothold with similarly inaccurate depictions of autism as seriously impaired boys whose disorder was worse than measles. Their advertising campaigns showed autism as a disease that destroyed families. Although Autism Speaks did offer a lot of resources for parents having difficulties managing their autistic children, their ad campaigns and depictions lacked the nuance necessary to show autism across the life span. All of these images of autism seeped into the global mindset and autism became synonymous with seriously disabled children who would lead a life with no meaning or purpose.

A Shift in Perspective

Quietly, without much fanfare, the clinical community changed their perspective on autism. In 2013, the *DSM-5* was released. In it, the three conditions of PDD-NOS, Asperger's syndrome, and ASD were acknowledged to be different levels of the same condition. However, media and public perception of autism stayed the same. This has made it difficult for people who don't have the original *DSM-3* depiction of autism to understand themselves, and because the clinical community remains susceptible to early depictions of autism as well, it has led to numerous misdiagnoses and misunderstandings. Many of us who are autistic have spent a lifetime hearing "you don't seem autistic to me" because misunderstandings about the nature and history of autism are part of the cultural mindset.

Popular culture has both helped and hurt this shift in perspective. Autistic people are now mainstays on shows like *The Big Bang Theory*, *Atypical*, and *The Good Doctor*. These depictions do show an increased understanding of autism as a spectrum that doesn't always present like the earlier *Rain Man* portrayal; however, they don't show the nuances and subtleties of presentation of autism across genders and the impact masking can have on the disorder.

Popular culture has embraced the idea of the spectrum as a linear concept that ranges across levels of assistance needed by autistic people rather than viewing the autism spectrum as a multifaceted presentation of behaviors. The increase of people saying things like "I am a little autistic" or "Aren't we all a little autistic?" spreads the idea that everyone can be somewhere on the autism spectrum. This is not true. The diagnostic criteria for autism in the current *DSM-5-TR* are quite rigid, but they can manifest in innumerable ways. Autism is defined by qualitative abnormalities in reciprocal social interaction, qualitative abnormalities in social communication, and restricted, repetitive, and hyperfixated patterns of behavior. This can look like many things, but all of the diagnostic criteria for autism must be met and must be evident in early childhood. However, the range of behavioral presentations means that you can "not seem autistic" to the general population and some clinicians who lack specific training in working with autistic adults and still very much meet diagnostic criteria for the disorder. This is the spectrum. So, the linear perspective of the autism spectrum going from low functioning to high functioning is wrong.

A little autistic   Very autistic

This following chart is the current preferred representation of the autism spectrum. This representation isn't entirely accurate and paints in broad strokes. Some details are missing but, in general, autism can be explained by a cluster of traits; understanding these traits is important to understanding yourself. The autism spectrum actually looks more like this.

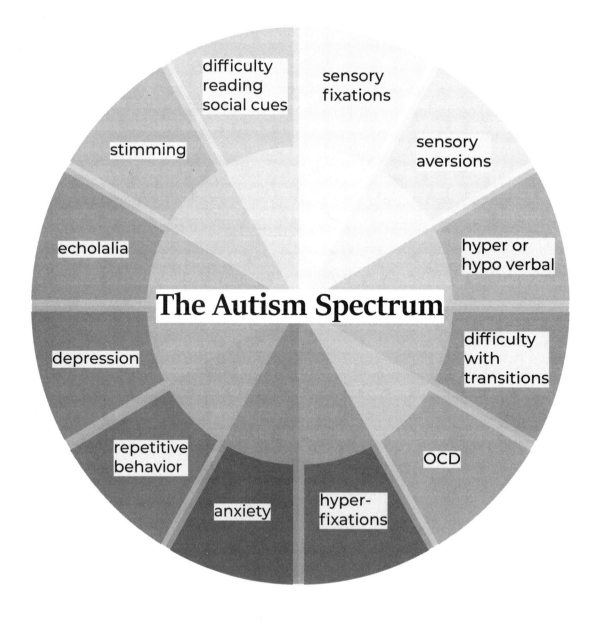

You may notice that there are things on this spectrum that are not part of the standard diagnostic criteria for autism. There are probably many things you have experienced that you know are pieces of your autism that are not seen in the *DSM* or on the standard depiction of the autism spectrum. There are a lot of other mental health issues that frequently overlap with autism, including depression, suicidality, ADHD, anxiety, gender dysphoria, and PTSD.

The spectrum makes treating and learning to cope with autism particularly difficult, because we are all so different. I may be high on echolalia, anxiety, strict adherence to sameness, and sensory aversions and fixations, and am hyperverbal. You may struggle with depression, hyperfixations, stimming, difficulty reading social cues, and difficulty with transitions. Still, even with these differences, we are both autistic.

Where You Fit on the Spectrum

In this chapter, you'll identify what you look like on the spectrum to decide which things you want to change and which things you want to keep. Just because you are autistic doesn't mean you should change anything or everything about yourself. As discussed in the previous chapter, there is nothing wrong with being an autistic person. However, if there are parts of you on this spectrum that cause anxiety or stress, you need specific neuro-affirmative tools to deal with them. The first step is identifying your autistic traits and deciding what your place on the spectrum looks like. The following exercise is also available online at http://www .newharbinger.com/53509.

YOUR PLACE ON THE SPECTRUM

On the following graph, highlight or draw your place on the spectrum. If you experience a particular trait more, indicate that by drawing your line closer to the outer circle. If you do not experience something as much, draw your line closer to the inner circle.

what it can actually look like:

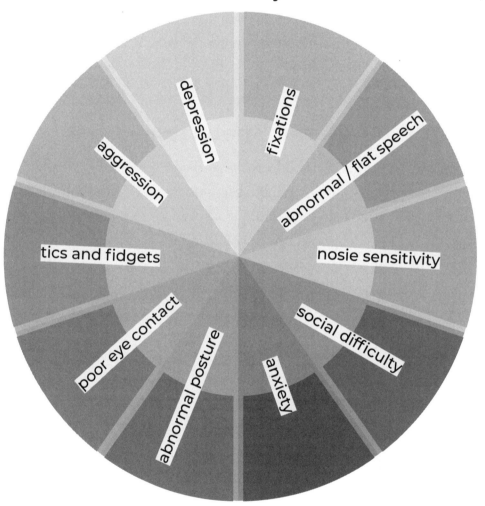

Where do you place yourself on the spectrum?

_____

_____

Which autistic traits cause you discomfort? Why?

_____

_____

_____

Which autistic traits do you love? Which ones would you never give up?

_____

_____

_____

_____

What Do You Want to Work On?

Now that you've identified which traits cause you discomfort and which traits you love, it's time to figure out which traits you want to work on. For example, I love my hyperfixated interests. I wrote three books about ghost stories when I went through a hyperfixation phase on ghosts. I love my sensory hyperfixations. I love getting entranced by a sunset or losing myself in the feeling of warm water or the softness of my dog's fur. In fact, I love most things about myself and my autistic traits. However, my meltdowns and shutdowns are exhausting and do damage to my daily life. Although stimming helps me, when my stimming gets so severe that I begin picking at myself until I bleed, that is a problem. Similarly, my getting overwhelmed and falling into echolaliac patterns when I am too anxious causes problems. I also want to work on recognizing social cues that might indicate that a situation is dangerous to me. My inability to notice other predatory humans has led to victimization and confusion in my life and I would love to learn to stop. I know my place on the spectrum and I also know that there are only four things I really want to work on to improve my quality of life. Let's look at some other examples.

Emma's Story

Emma came to see me for autism testing when she was twenty-four. She met all the diagnostic criteria but testing revealed her strength was communication and she was off the chart in hyperfixated and rigid interests and stereotyped behaviors. She learned to talk at ten months old and was hyperverbal, but she missed social cues and often said inappropriate things that offended people at the wrong time. Others saw her as pretentious or rude. In private, she tended to repeat the same words and got agitated when anything in her home was moved or her schedule changed. She collected rocks she found in random places and bits of shiny glass. She also collected yarn and loved knitting, and she spent hours studying yarn and different knitting techniques. Even when she wasn't knitting it occupied her thoughts. She worked to mask most of these traits, but this caused her stress and anxiety.

After working in therapy, Emma could see that her social impairments caused her the most stress and that loneliness and depression were the parts of autism she wanted to work on. She also decided to work on loving herself as she was and finding a few people she could feel safe with. Emma loved that her stimming offered her comfort when she was stressed, and she wanted to keep that. She also loved her passion for knitting and rock collecting, so she wanted to use those hyperfixations as ways to cope with her anxiety, but she chose to learn the spoons technique to avoid meltdowns.

Can you relate to any elements of Emma's story?

_____

_____

_____

While autistic meltdown and shutdown likely cause you discomfort, they are not on this spectrum chart. Both states occur when autistic people are so overwhelmed by sensory experiences or environmental demands that they can no longer function. These states are usually secondary to other parts of autism. Their occurrence makes sense when you look at neurological studies of autistic people versus controls. A study by Kenown (2013) found that autistic people show "widespread local overconnectivity in ASD," and that this overconnectivity is linked to overwhelm, resulting in meltdown and shutdown. Meltdown occurs when a buildup of stress and anxiety results in an unwanted behavioral outburst that usually feels out of control and may include yelling, crying, sobbing, and, in extreme cases, self-injury or injury to others. Shutdown occurs when the built-up stress and anxiety becomes so overwhelming that the autistic person just shuts off. Early studies of this showed autistic children would become almost completely catatonic, but it can also look like slowed movement and speech, an inability to talk, or seeking a quiet place. In almost all cases, the goal is to avoid entering either of these states and if they are entered to find healthy ways to accept them and let them pass. They can rarely be prevented once they have begun.

Mark's Story

Mark started therapy because he was told by his wife that he wasn't empathetic enough and he was too blunt. After a few sessions, he was tested for autism and had notably high traits in all diagnostic criteria. Mark had been delayed in speech and walking as a child and went to speech and physical therapy for both things. He had been in gifted classes as a child, and he excelled in all subjects. He was a software engineer and had friends through an online video game he played. He was quiet and reserved. He collected Magic: The Gathering cards and had made a few friends through this in high school, but he later lost those friendships. He reported struggling his entire life with people and had lost several jobs due to interpersonal conflicts. He didn't understand why his wife was mad at him all the time and tended to retreat to his study when she was angry. He also indicated he had been bullied a lot in grade school and middle school and had trauma symptoms from this. He worked from home and became anxious about any real-world interactions with people.

Mark decided that he wanted to work on his childhood trauma, dual empathy solutions, and better communication with his wife. He also wanted to work on flexibility and learn coping skills to deal with transitions to improve his relationship with his wife. Because he wanted to be able to change jobs, he also wanted to discuss how to better navigate groups of people in meetings and at work. He wanted to keep his stimming, hyperfixations, sensory aversions, and love of order because he didn't see how these damaged anything and they were more helpful than harmful. In the end, we worked on dual empathy with his wife and unmasking skills for work.

_____

_____

_____

Common Traits of Autistic People That Aren't Diagnostic

Just like with meltdown and shutdown, which are not specifically autism traits, there are many struggles common to autistic people that might not be labeled as such. They are not diagnostic but are the parts of the spectrum that hide in the cracks. Do you have any struggles with autism that aren't normally part of the diagnostic criteria? Circle any items that apply to you:

- **Eating disorders:** Anorexia, bulimia, and overeating are among many possible eating disorders.

- **Rejection sensitive dysphoria:** This is when you experience severe emotional pain because of a failure or feeling rejected. It is common to both ADHD and autism. This is believed to be caused by differences in brain structure.

- **Pathological demand avoidance:** This is the tendency of neurodivergent people to avoid any demands or stressors that trigger anxiety or sensory overload to a much more significant degree than the normal population.

- **Auditory processing disorder:** This is a disorder that impacts our ability to understand speech. The sounds can be heard but the brain misinterprets sounds. People who struggle with this may radically misinterpret what is said by others or may just misunderstand things. The four auditory processing skills people with this disorder struggle with are 1) distinguishing between separate sounds, 2) being able to separate sound from background noise, 3) remembering what has been heard, and 4) understanding the order sounds are heard in.

- **Sensory processing disorder:** This is similar to auditory process disorder in that it is a disorder in the way the brain perceives and understands sensory input. People with this disorder have difficulty filtering and knowing which sensory information is important and which they should respond to. Everything can be overwhelming or underwhelming.

- **Poor posture:** This is a body position that is asymmetrical or atypical.

- **Lack of organizational skills:** This is an inability to prioritize tasks, manage time effectively, set goals, and juggle multiple responsibilities.

- **Obsessive-compulsive disorder (OCD):** This is defined as recurring thoughts and obsessions and behaviors and compulsions that you feel you must repeat over and over again. It is normal for autistic people to have stereotyped and repetitive behavior. This differs from obsessions and compulsions in that most stereotyped behavior and stimming for autistic people alleviates anxiety. With OCD, it is like being trapped in a loop of anxiety you cannot escape.

- **Depression:** Most autistic people have at least one episode of depression in their life. Loneliness, anxiety, trauma, and isolation can contribute to depression in autistic people. Symptoms of depression can include decreased mood for more days than not over a prolonged period, sleep problems, and appetite changes.

- **Being quickly overwhelmed:** This is feeling overcome by a deluge of simple tasks, activities, or stimuli.

- **Social anxiety:** This is extreme anxiety in social situations.

- **Generalized anxiety disorder:** This is a sense of constant anxiety that occurs more days than not over an extended time. There are many reasons for autistic adults to struggle with generalized anxiety. Isolation, not being able to read social cues, not understanding various communication styles, rejection, loneliness, and isolation can all contribute to generalized anxiety.

- **Overthinking:** This is ruminating or fixating on thoughts.

- **Alexithymia:** This is an inability to understand your own emotions and your own inner state. Autistic people often struggle with questions like "How are you?"

- **PTSD and trauma from toxic relationships:** Symptoms of PTSD can include nightmares, flashbacks, severe anxiety, distrust, insomnia, dissociation, guilt, depression, and hypervigilance.

- **Masking/camouflaging:** This is the tendency of autistic people to observe the social behaviors of neurotypicals and take on the traits and personas of those around them to try to blend in with and be accepted by neurotypical society. It has been shown to cause increased anxiety, depression, and suicidality. It is often the end product of social skills training or environments that stigmatize and force conformity.

- **Dissociation:** This is the tendency to enter an autonomic shutdown state and retreat into worlds of fantasy or cognitively leave your own body. Autistic people tend to do this more deeply than neurotypicals. The data show that the early hypotheses of autism being genius without imagination are wrong.

- **Having different personalities for different situations**

- **Clumsiness:** Autistic people may have difficulty with coordination and gross and fine motor skills. In extreme cases, autistic people can have disorders like dysautonomia or Meniere's disease, which leads to difficulties with balance and frequent falling.

- **Executive dysfunction:** This occurs impairment in cognitive abilities result in difficulties with attention, memory, and movement between tasks.

None of these things are diagnostic in and of themselves, but if you are autistic, you probably have wrestled with at least one of these issues on a regular basis. Many of them are disorders unto themselves, but as you begin to understand yourself it is important to know what some of these things are.

Have you struggled with any of the items on the list above? Which ones and how has this affected your life?

_____

_____

_____

_____

_____

_____

_____

Now it's time to bring all the information you have learned about yourself so far in this chapter and organize it in one place. Here are some techniques to help you facilitate this. These two exercises are also available online at http://www.newharbinger.com/53509.

WHAT IS A GIFT?

What parts or your autism do you love?	What need does this fulfill?
Ex. I love my stimming.	It helps me let out emotions that are overwhelming. I am not comfortable doing it too much publicly, but it helps.
Ex. I love my info-dumps.	They are a source of unending joy I am happy to do publicly and privately.

What parts or your autism do you love?	What need does this fulfill?

WHAT DO YOU NEED HELP WITH?

What are the parts of autism that cause you difficulty?	How does this prevent you from doing something important?
Ex. I struggle with social interactions.	This prevents me from making long-term friendships and engaging in work-related activities that require small talk and conversation.
Ex. I have auditory processing disorder.	I love Halloween. I want to learn to make it through Halloween nights without being overwhelmed by sensory experience.

What are the parts of autism that cause you difficulty?	How does this prevent you from doing something important?

These two charts will be your template for change while using this workbook and if you decide to enter therapy. The parts of yourself you love and consider strengths you should never change, even if others have been cruel to you about them. They are you and you are perfect the way you are. The parts of you that you struggle with shouldn't be changed entirely either, but by using the tools in this workbook you may find ways to cope with them, accept them, or learn to change them a little bit so that you can be more comfortable having them in your day-to-day life.

CHAPTER 4

Accepting Your Disability Needs

You may or may not see autism as a disability. There are different ways of perceiving ASD, and a lot depends on whether the discussion is coming from a neurotypical perspective—which tends to be a medical point of view—or from the perspective of those of us who are autistic. Many autistic adults and autism advocates describe autism as a different type of brain functioning and a different way of relating to the world. In this chapter, we'll look at this closely. I invite you to engage the writing prompts to explore your own way of thinking about your autism. Let's start with three definitions that people commonly use to describe the diagnosis.

The Centers for Disease Control (CDC) describes autism spectrum disorder as a "developmental disability that is caused by differences in how the brain functions. Autistic people may communicate, interact, behave, and learn in different ways."

The Americans with Disabilities Act (ADA) defines a person with a disability as someone who has a physical or mental impairment that substantially limits one or more major life activities. Keeping this in mind, an autistic person is defined as someone whose difficulties with communication, behavior, and socialization contribute to impairment that substantially limits one or more major life activities.

The Diagnostic and Statistical Manual of Mental Disorders (DSM) describes autism in terms of levels of disability, which we'll look at more closely later in the chapter.

How Autism Limits People

There are two major ways that autism has been found to limit people: in school and at work. In the school system, autistic children are routinely put in special education programs regardless of their intellectual functioning because their behaviors make it very difficult for them to assimilate into rigid neurotypical classrooms. Data show that employment rates among autistic individuals are low and that job retention for autistic adults is even lower. According to Harmuth et al. (2018), "At an individual level, poor social communication and interpersonal skills are commonly reported as challenges to gaining and maintaining employment." In an article for *Harvard Business Review*, Praslova (2021) concludes that many people who are neurodivergent are "bullied, exploited, or underpaid." She goes on to describe people being rejected or fired after disclosing that they are autistic.

Do you struggle with job retention? Describe when you have been bullied, exploited, or underpaid at work.

_____

_____

_____

_____

_____

On the other hand, advocates argue that autism itself isn't a disability but rather neurotypical society's inability to cope with the differences of autism. All the descriptions you read about the things that define why autism is a disability in and of itself are based on structures created and defined by neurotypicals. What are poor social skills? Lack of eye contact? Inability to engage in small talk? Lack of to-and-fro conversation? All these things are only necessary because they make neurotypicals more comfortable in job environments. In most cases, they have nothing to do with job performance in and of itself.

What traits of autism have limited you at school or work? Do you feel your difficulty at school or work has anything to do with what's actually needed to perform your school- or work-related tasks or other things? What are the other things?

_____

_____

_____

_____

According to Praslova (2021), autistic professionals can be up to 140 percent more productive than the typical employee. Yet underemployment or unemployment remains the critical indicator that justifies the idea that autism is a disability. Between that and the need for special services in neurotypical schools, it is easy to say that it is a disability…or at least it is easy to say we have a mental difference that substantially limits major life activities.

Despite all of this, I agree with autism advocates who say that autism in and of itself isn't a disability. When the stressors of conforming to neurotypical expectations are removed, most of us can accomplish as much, if not more, than any neurotypical. I climbed Mt. Kilimanjaro while I was pregnant. I ran a marathon. I have backpacked and traveled and written ten books, but I did all these things alone, free of neurotypical demands. The problems arise when we are forced to live in a world that wasn't designed for us, when we need to interact with normal society and function within parameters that don't fit the way we thrive. The research shows that we can be hardworking, innovative, and insightful, all assets to work environments. Autistic people can be exceptional if they are placed in environments that are flexible enough to meet their needs. A fish can't thrive in a tree, and it is ridiculous to think it can.

How have you been forced to adapt to a society that wasn't designed for you?

Write about how you had to adapt in school: _____

_____

_____

_____

_____

Write about how you had to adapt at work: _____

_____

_____

_____

_____

Consider that since we must adapt to neurotypical society and the data show that it is difficult for us to adapt to do so, we may need to let go of semantics and accept the fact that in the current societal structure, autism is disabling. It is disabling because we are forced to live in societies that don't bend or change to help us thrive. We are forced to work in jobs where networking and social skills matter, even if we are engineers or surgeons and talking to people isn't integral to our job functioning. Our employers will judge us on our lack of eye contact even if we are at the top of our field. Our colleagues will expect us to network even if it causes us panic. We will be expected to conform to nine-to-five jobs and follow rigid hours even if we work best working sixty hours one week and twenty hours the next and get twice as much work done as our coworkers. We will be expected to give presentations, smile, have seamless executive functioning, dress right, and act right, not because it is part of the job but because being normal is important to neurotypicals. All of this makes autism a disability.

How has autism been disabling for you? What do you naturally want to do that you can't, because society won't let you?

_____

_____

_____

_____

_____

You must accept this disability not because I believe you are disabled but because you know it will always be ten times harder for you to survive in this society than a neurotypical. By embracing the semantics of this word, you can give yourself allowances to get the help you need when you need it.

That doesn't mean we shouldn't fight to change this in the long run, but it does mean that you need to learn to cope with the things that make autism disabling for you so that you can have a higher quality of life. So, when I talk about learning to accept your disability, I mean learning to accept that you will have difficulty navigating the neurotypical world and that it is okay to admit that it is preventing you from having a high quality of life. You shouldn't ever believe that there is anything wrong with you or with being autistic any more than a fish should admit there is something wrong with it because it is being forced to live on land. Let's continue to look at Emma's story.

Emma's Story

Emma suspected she was autistic. She had seen TikTok videos about autism and she felt that her experiences were like the women she saw online. Emma was a thirty-year-old woman who had moved back in with her parents after a divorce. Her marriage had been traumatic, and she had endured physical and emotional abuse, but she blamed herself for being too "weird" for anyone to handle. Emma had no friends and rarely left the house. She liked knitting and crocheting and spent most of her day sleeping or making beautiful yarn creations.

She had struggled throughout her schooling, and although she could excel in classes like art, she failed math and science. She had been on a 504B plan in school because she lost things and couldn't pay attention. She also had auditory processing disorder and had trouble understanding what people said, as well as dysautonomia, or difficulty with balance and proprioception. These things made school impossible for her. Her parents had eventually homeschooled her for the last three years of high school. She hadn't held a job for more than a year despite numerous attempts.

Emma tended to beat herself up for her inability to hold a job. She hated herself and criticized herself harshly for not living up to neurotypical expectations. Emma was not good at speaking and was nonspeaking at various times in her life. To help her and to respect her communication style, our sessions were all done via written exchanges in my office. I wrote the questions, and she answered them in writing. She was a beautiful and brilliant writer.

Testing showed that Emma was amazing at puzzle completion and topped out certain aspects of IQ tests but her working memory score and her concrete thinking made her overall IQ 82. Emma was exceptional at many tasks, but she couldn't keep a job or live on her own. Emma "didn't seem autistic" to most people, but follow-up testing with a psychologist and with vocational rehab showed that Emma was level 2 autistic. She also had major depressive disorder, generalized anxiety disorder, posttraumatic stress disorder, auditory processing disorder, and ADHD. Vocational rehab declared her disability to be too high for her to maintain any job placement they could get her. Emma ended up getting full disability.

Even after she was given disability status, she had trouble accepting her disability. In the school system, teachers had called her lazy and told her she just didn't put in the effort to do well. Her husband had told her she was lazy and useless. She had faced a lifetime of criticism and it was hard for her to believe that she had been genuinely trying as hard as she could for most of her life. As an autistic person, she just couldn't keep up with neurotypical job expectations.

After a few years, she was able turn her passion for yarn into a side venture that brought her a little extra income. She made little yarn creatures and sold them via local venders and online. This gave her a sense of purpose and improved her quality of life. People admired her skills, and her little creatures were remarkable. I still marvel at their beautiful intricacy. Although she doesn't have any friends in real life, she doesn't want any and is most comfortable alone. She is active in a few online groups and that is enough for her.

Do you, like Emma, criticize yourself for your difficulties fitting into neurotypical society? If so, how?

_____

_____

_____

_____

_____

Levels of Support Needed

The level to which autistic people struggle in neurotypical society varies significantly. Some people are fully and completely disabled while some have less restrictive disabilities. Although most of us don't like functioning labels because none of us feels "high functioning," some of us require more support than others. The *DSM-5-TR* explains this in levels of care needed. I have summed up these support level needs to help you understand where your support needs might be.

Level 1: Requiring Support	At level 1, autistic people struggle to understand and comply with social cues, rules, and conventions. They may have difficulty making and maintaining friendships. They may struggle with communication and understanding others and being understood. They may have hyperfixated interests, experience stress during transitions, and engage in stimming. At this level, children will need accommodations like extra time for tests, noise-canceling headphones, and quiet time. Adults may struggle with obtaining and maintaining employment.
Level 2: Requiring Substantial Support	At this level, speech and social behavior are more noticeably different. Autistic people at this level might need to be in special education or have an educational aide with them in school. They may need speech and occupational therapy. As adults, they may not be able to obtain or maintain employment and may require disability.
Level 3: Requiring Very Substantial Support	At this level, autistic people visibly appear very "autistic." They may be nonspeaking or have echolalia. At this level, they may need special education and will not be able to obtain or maintain employment. They may need daily help in their living environment or need a regular caretaker. They may never be able to live or function on their own.

Most people reading this book will fall into the level 1 or level 2 range of support requirements. It is important to note that even people within level 1 need support. Functioning in a society that is not designed for you is difficult at every level.

What level of support do you need? Write about some of the things you struggle with that are described in the different levels.

_____

_____

_____

_____

Let's start looking at your needs for support. As we begin this process, the first question you must ask is what challenges limit your life activities. I struggle to be in new places that have too much happening. I am very sensitive to sensory stimuli, and it takes very little noise, light, and movement for me to be completely overwhelmed. This can be too many people, too much talking, too much noise, too many items in a store with too many colors or too many smells. Chaotic places with unpredictable variables like the grocery store can shut me down. I haven't been in a grocery store alone in ten years. This is a disability for me because I need food. The following exercise is also available online at http://www.newharbinger.com/53509.

YOUR SUPPORT NEEDS

What is your disability?	How does this make your life a struggle?
Ex. I have difficulty making the appropriate facial expression at the right time.	People often misinterpret my actions, which leads to people being put off by me. It makes it difficult for me to interact with other moms at school, with other professionals, and with other humans in general. It makes networking, keeping jobs, and parenting hard.
Ex. I get overwhelmed and shut down periodically. I can work for sixty to eighty hours for months and then I shut down and need a break.	I haven't ever been able to hold a standard nine-to-five job for more than two years.

What is your disability?	How does this make your life a struggle?

Respecting Your Disability

You may have found ways to adapt to societal expectations. Some of these adaptations may feel unnatural or cause you extra effort, and because people don't understand the need for them, you may hide these behaviors. To admit this, even just to yourself, is a way of respecting your disability.

For the most part, I am a very successful woman. If you didn't look closely, you would call me a "very high-functioning adult." I have been told that I "don't seem autistic" by many people. People also say, "You do so well for an autistic person." They comment on how successful I seem.

Yet, if they were to look deeper, they'd realize things are more complex for me. I haven't gone to the grocery store alone in ten years. I have a service dog to help me leave the house on my own. If I hadn't designed a private practice to be accommodating to my disability, I would have trouble maintaining full-time employment. The longest time I was able to hold a full-time, regular job was two years, when I worked at a clinic and tried very hard to be social, blend in, and do and say what I thought was normal in that environment. I mimicked other people's behaviors and tried to be like them. I engaged in behaviors I found aversive, like gossiping, to try to appear normal. I worked relentlessly hard and was promoted, but it was exhausting. After a year and a half, the anxiety, depression, and tatters in my masking abilities led to a complete meltdown. All of this could have been prevented if I had respected my disability and known my limitations.

I am disabled within the context of neurotypical society, and I am comfortable admitting this. I am even comfortable celebrating it at times. I love who I am and I wouldn't change any of it. This is my form of respecting myself.

Do you appear more adapted to neurotypical society than you are? What disabilities and hardships have you hidden?

_____

_____

_____

How comfortable or uncomfortable are you with using the word "disability"? Write your thoughts down.

_____

_____

_____

_____

Asking for Help

Admitting your hardships matters, and admitting the help you need matters. You don't have to use the word "disability," but admitting that a fish living on land will need special help is important. You are trying to live in a world that doesn't fit you. Because of that, you may not be able to live up to neurotypical norms and you will probably need extra help. I have admitted I need a service animal and I can now get the help I need to survive in a neurotypical world. My service dog allows me to go hiking, visit art exhibitions, and travel. I can backpack. I can live a full life. He helps me at work. I have asked friends to help me go to the grocery store and now I am able to get groceries and cook for my family. Going into private practice and allowing myself to take days off when I am melting down or shutting down has allowed me to maintain steady employment for seven years. All this is possible because I respect my disability. I respect my unique needs and I don't try to pretend I can function like neurotypicals.

Do any of the following statements resonate with you? Do you find them empowering, soothing, or disturbing?

- *I am not like other people and that is okay.*

- *I need extra help and that is okay.*

- *I am still a hard worker even though I can't operate in traditional work environments.*

- *I can be helpful and still need help.*

Write down the thoughts you have about these statements.

_____

_____

_____

Write your own empowering statement.

_____

_____

These are the messages you need to tell yourself every day because your quality of life matters. You deserve the same things as neurotypicals do. Just because fish need water instead of air doesn't mean fish don't have the right to breathe. You deserve a work environment that is comfortable. You deserve a life in which you can be comfortable, feel safe, and be your best self. To achieve these things, you may need to ask for help. Jacob's story is an example of how one of my clients asked for help. Let's explore how asking for help changed the trajectory of his college experience.

Jacob's Story

Jacob has always struggled with social interactions and even though he was able to make straight As and had won numerous awards in art class, he couldn't figure out why everyone thought he was weird, difficult, and at times "mean." He hoped going to art school would be a fresh start for him.

He left for college and things got worse. The social pressures of constantly being with other people were debilitating. He still couldn't make friends and he didn't understand what he was doing wrong. He was failing any class that wasn't art-related and was risking losing his scholarship.

Jacob went to disability services at the university and they gave him extra help. He was given extended time for taking tests, a special quiet place for test taking, extended deadlines for assignments, and tutoring. With the decrease in pressure, Jacob was able to stabilize and return his grades to his usual straight As. He ended up finding a Dungeons and Dragons group on campus that met regularly and joined several other gaming clubs. He still struggled with people in other environments, but finding a few stable friendships and reducing the pressures of neurotypical performance needs in class allowed him to thrive in college.

Jacob learned to ask for help from school when he needed it. Have there been times in your life when you could have made things easier by asking for help? List those times.

_____

_____

_____

_____

There is beauty in what makes you different and strength in what other people don't understand. Take a minute to look at how you can ask for help to improve your quality of life.

Use the chart below to evaluate where you need help and what help you need. This exercise is also available online at http://www.newharbinger.com/53509.

WHAT KIND OF HELP DO YOU NEED?

What is your disability?	What help can you get that will improve your quality of life?
Ex. I struggle to work jobs that require regular social interaction and a nine-to-five schedule.	I moved into private practice with a more flexible schedule.
Ex. I have trouble going to public places that are loud, crowded, and overwhelming.	I have a service dog.

Neuro-Affirmative Therapy

This is a relatively new concept. Historically, autism treatment has always focused on changing behavior to blend in with normative society. Neuro-affirmative therapy is almost the opposite of that. It is therapy that embraces and accepts your differences. If you are in neuro-affirmative therapy, you are with a therapist or psychiatrist who respects your autism and doesn't try to teach you neurotypical social skills. Instead, they work with you to help you find solutions to your problems while also respecting yourself. This doesn't mean you won't be asked to change self-destructive behaviors or pushed to learn new coping skills, but it does mean that you will be celebrated for your uniqueness and that uniqueness will be integrated into your treatment plan as a strength and not a weakness. Treatment modalities will focus on treating your co-occurring conditions and working with you to unmask and embrace your strengths.

Therapies I have used that have worked very well with autism include internal family systems, the Safe and Sound Protocol, dialectic behavioral therapy, autism coaching, gaming therapy, mindfulness-focused therapies, and Jungian analysis. Although cognitive behavioral therapy (CBT) is one of the most popular and empirically backed therapies available for treatment of most mental health concerns, I have found it can have mixed results with autism.

Most autistic adults will need therapy at various points in their lives. It is more important for autistic adults to research their therapists than most people. Almost every therapist and psychiatrist is trained in dealing with depression and anxiety, but very few have been trained in dealing with autism. If you follow my Discord server and online groups, I try to keep up with neuro-affirmative therapists in different areas.

Autism as a Superpower

In 2009, Autism Speaks began an advertisement campaign that got things so wrong, it galvanized many autism advocates to come forward and stand up. The advertisement that led this campaign was triggering and heartbreaking for anyone who is autistic. In this grim, black-and-white advertisement, the voice-over says, "I am autism. I work faster than pediatric AIDS, cancer, and diabetes combined and if you are happily married, I will make sure your marriage fails. I will bankrupt you for my own selfish gain. I don't sleep, so I make sure you don't either. I will make it virtually impossible for your family to attend the temple, birthday party, or public park without embarrassment or shame." The advertisement is quite long and paints autism as a hidden monster that sucks the soul from family and humanity. It "plots to rob you of your family and your dreams."

The reaction to this advertisement campaign from the autistic community and autism advocates was powerful. It was a cry in the dark that just because we are autistic doesn't mean we are nothing but "embarrassment and shame." In direct response to this, many autistic people and their supporters stepped forward and proclaimed that autism is a "superpower." They said we aren't a disease. We aren't disabled. We won't bankrupt our families or destroy marriages. This shift was a necessary and pivotal change. It was critical that researchers, professionals, and autistic people stopped viewing autism through the lens of parents who had difficult children. At some point, the world needed to wake up and realize that autistic adults exist and that autistic people deserve a voice of their own.

Autism can be a superpower. According to Uddin (2022), "A small but significant portion of individuals diagnosed as autistic exhibit exceptional cognitive abilities in one or more domains. These twice-exceptional individuals often have unique skills that potentially enable them to make significant contributions to the workforce, but at the same time face unique challenges during the transition to independent living because of lack of services and broad public misperceptions regarding their condition."

Meilleur, Jelenic, and Mottron (2015) found that as many as 60 percent of autistic people have special isolated skills. These special abilities are predictive of our ability to function in neurotypical society, but they aren't predictive of our disability in general. Also, the concept of autistic superpowers is far more complex than the rhetoric would make you think. For example, in Uddin's et al.'s research, they had to break the "superpowers" down into subgroups. They describe people who are twice exceptional and have higher cognitive functioning, IQs, and special abilities and people who have cognitive divergence. Some people have special abilities but profound deficits in other areas. They also describe savant syndrome in which an individual has an island of ability in a sea of deficits. It is also important to note that according to this research, 40 percent of autistic people have no special isolated skills and lower cognitive functioning. So, although autism can be a superpower, it is universally a disability in the current social structure, as research shows that even those who are twice exceptional have to struggle with other hardships that come with autism, such as social and communication difficulties.

So, although I love this narrative of autism as a superpower and I love that those of us who are autism self-advocates are fighting the narrative that autism is a disability that destroys lives, it can be problematic to only focus on the superpower aspect of autism. I am lucky. I am twice exceptional. I have the best-case scenario as far as autistic people go, but I still struggle; failing to acknowledge these struggles can create difficulties for people who need help.

It is also not fair to the many people who don't have any "special abilities" to call autism a superpower. Many people only struggle, and it is hard for them to see the superpower aspect of autism. For those who only get the hardship that comes with autism, accepting the label of disability allows them to reach out for the help they so desperately need. Still, if you have superpowers or gifts, you need to celebrate them. Even if the gifts are small, they are worth celebrating. Think of Emma, who could create beautiful yarn animals. Every gift counts.

Take a minute and celebrate your gifts, even the small ones. Even the ones others don't see.

_____

_____

_____

_____

Accepting the Disability Isn't Always About Neurotypical Society

I am at a beautiful point in my life where people try to respect my disability and my special needs most of the time. People love me and listen to me. Yet, I still struggle. It isn't that neurotypical society doesn't make space for me and doesn't try to have empathy for me. Sometimes, it is just that autism makes my life more difficult.

This was clear when I tried to go to my son's track meet. He needed my support and everyone at the meet welcomed me and my service dog. They worked hard to make my son and I feel safe. However, it was loud. There were hundreds of kids and all the parents there were working as hard as they could to organize events, which were announced on the loud-speaker. It was hot. Kids were laughing and yelling. People were everywhere. Even though everyone tried, I had to leave and there was nothing anyone could have done for me more than they did. It was too hot and too loud and too chaotic for me.

Sometimes I struggle because I am easily overwhelmed; sometimes it has nothing to do with anyone but me, and I must learn to cope with it on my own. It isn't about asking others for help. It is about asking myself to be prepared for things I know I will struggle with. I should have known the track meet would be hard. I could have brought noise-canceling headphones. I could have brought a fan and umbrella to keep the sun off me. These were ways I failed to respect my own disability.

So here is the final challenge: to remember your limitations and prepare for those limitations in advance. What are your limitations? How can you prepare for them? Use the chart below to think about these questions. This exercise is also available online at http://www.newharbinger.com/53509.

PREPARING FOR LIMITATIONS

What are your limitations?	When are they problematic?	How can you prepare for the problematic times?
Ex. I have difficulty in loud, crowded, overwhelming places.	In busy public places	I can remember I need noise-canceling headphones, my dog, a few fidget toys to help me relax, and an escape plan in case I have to leave.

What are your limitations?	When are they problematic?	How can you prepare for the problematic times?

In the end, what is most important to remember is that it is okay that you are different, and you should embrace that and find ways to give yourself comfort and safety in environments that are difficult for you. Your comfort matters.

The pressure to fit in to neurotypical society can cause significant anxiety. Most autism advocates argue that society should try harder to make space for us. However, I believe much of the pressure comes from within us. We feel compelled to try to make others happy and try to belong in a world we have always felt out of place in. Yet quality of life comes when you let go of neurotypical expectations and embrace your weird. Find the beauty in your weirdness and make it part of what defines you despite neurotypical expectations.

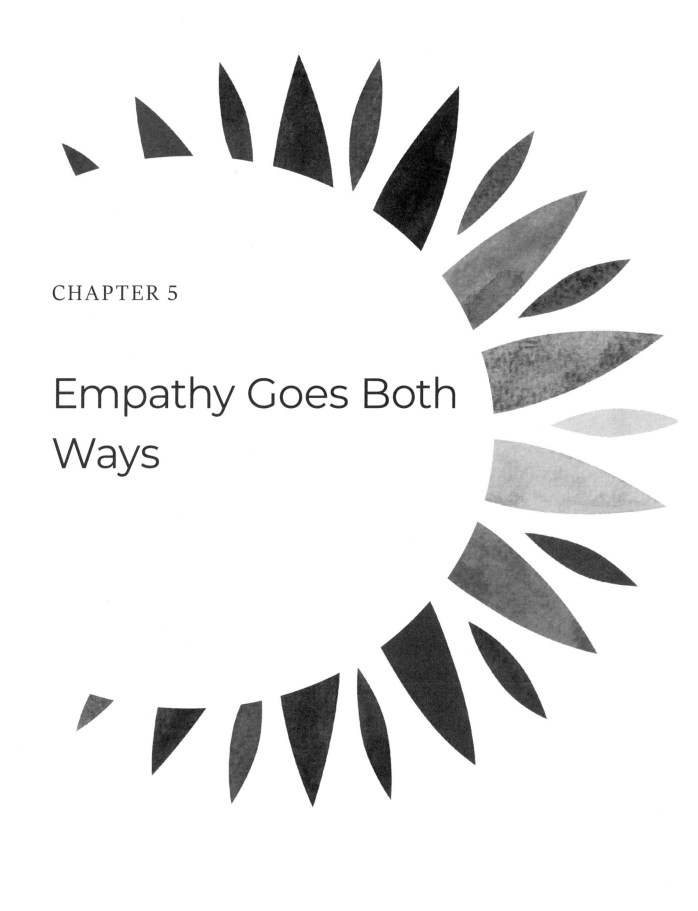

CHAPTER 5

Empathy Goes Both Ways

What if the problem with social interactions for autistic people doesn't rest solely in their "abnormalities in social interaction" but rather in a dual problem, where we are equally misunderstood? The double empathy problem is a theory that suggests that the problem also rests with neurotypicals. Just as autistic people struggle to have empathy for neurotypicals, neurotypicals struggle to have empathy for autistic people. It isn't just that autistic people are terrible at social interactions. It is that the way neurotypicals and autistic people relate to the world is so different that it is difficult for us to have empathy for each other.

This concept was first introduced by Milton (2012) and research supports this idea. According to Alkhaldi et al. (2021), neurotypical people misperceive autistic people and "like" neurotypical people better. Not only do neurotypicals not like autistic people but they also find us less attractive and less trustworthy. According to Mitchell and Pearce (2021), neurotypicals' responses to and perceptions of autistic people are usually negative and lead to people becoming isolated from society. According to Crompton and Davis (2021), autistic people are better at interacting with each other and "research indicates that autistic people are less likely to rely on typical social expectations for interacting or be upset if such expectations are not followed."

Although these facts might seem intuitive to someone who has lived their entire life as an autistic person, they are critical. They mean that we can interact with each other without the problems we encounter with neurotypicals. They also mean that if we can learn neurotypicals, it isn't impossible for neurotypicals to learn us too. Up until this point, the primary treatment for autism is to try to change us to make us more palatable for neurotypicals. The suggestion embedded in this theory is that instead of the bats being forced to live like birds, the birds will like us as we are. Perhaps the birds and that bats should begin to respect each other. Perhaps we should take time and learn each other's unique social styles. The demand shouldn't be put entirely on the bats to act more like birds, but rather for us both to have empathy for each other and accept each other as the unique creatures we are.

What things would you like neurotypicals to understand about you?

_____

_____

_____

If you were to give neurotypicals social skills training to help them relate to you, what would you teach them?

_____

_____

_____

_____

_____

The Problem with Double Empathy

In a perfect world, the goal would be double empathy, with neurotypicals and autistic people striving to communicate and understand each other. The problem is, double empathy doesn't exist. Our culture very clearly trains autistic children from an early age that we are the ones that need to learn neurotypical social skills and that our intrinsic socials skills are broken and wrong. So, despite the fact that our social skills are sufficient when we interact with other neurodivergent people, we are expected to learn new skills, and neurotypicals bear no burden of learning us.

I love following the myriad of #actuallyautistic Instagram, TikTok, and other online influencers who boldly talk about their lived experiences as autistic people. They offer such a source of support for people struggling with finding community. They also offer people like me insight into the diversity of experiences autistic people have. One of the autism advocates I follow goes by the online name Fun Facts with Lulu. In a recent Instagram post she said, "I want to see way less 'how to unmask as an autistic' and way way way more 'how to make the spaces you have power over less dangerous and more safe for autistic people to be themselves.'" I love this because it sums up the double empathy problem. The problem is that neurotypicals have no drive to makes spaces better for us, so it is up to us to figure out how to have a happy life around their weird rules and structures and hope that our advocacy work will help the next generation.

If neurotypicals were to create a society that was more designed for you to thrive in, what would that look like? Be as creative as you want. You might get out a sheet of paper and draw it.

_____

_____

_____

_____

_____

The large question in this chapter is how do we cope with the double empathy problem? How do we thrive in a world in which we are different without sacrificing who we are? This is important, despite socialization and the social skills training messages in our society, because we can't sacrifice who we are to solve this problem.

Individualization

According to Carl Jung (2003), "By individualization I mean the psychological process that makes of a human being an 'individual'—a unique, indivisible unit or 'whole man.'" According to Jungian philosophy, this is the goal of therapy. The goal is to find and be yourself. Jung is not a modern, empirically driven psychologist, but his philosophy holds some universal truths. Loving yourself for who you are brings inner peace. Self-esteem is an important predictor of subjective well-being. Loving ourselves as individuals is important.

It may seem odd that we start a chapter that is ultimately about relationships and human interaction with the concept of individualization and self-esteem, but according to Jung, "the process of individualization does not shut one out from the world but gathers the world to them." Essentially this means that we can't have healthy relationships by sacrificing ourselves as individuals. The more we are content with who we are, the stronger and more authentic our relationships will become.

Despite this, social skills training teaches you to live a lie. It teaches you to sacrifice yourself and your needs to conform to neurotypical needs and desires. This may make you superficially more likable, but it will also make you vulnerable to predatory people and to relationships with massive boundary violations, and it will drive away healthy people who want genuine connectivity in a relationship with others.

So, the first step in forming real relationships is to begin understanding yourself as an individual and respecting your individual needs and values. For example, I had a client who entered a friendship with a woman who loved romantic movies and running. My client didn't like either of these things nor did she think gossip was ethical. Yet, to make her friend happy, she watched romance movies and began running. She listened to and engaged in gossip while smiling and mimicking the behaviors of her new friend. Her new friend was happy for a while, but eventually the relationship dissolved because it was too stressful for my client to maintain and the friend violated her boundaries so often that it was damaging to her. If she prioritized herself as an individual, on the other hand, she would seek out friendships in which she was comfortable stating her likes and dislikes clearly. She would engage in activities she and her friend both enjoyed and they would learn and respect each other's boundaries.

My clients are sometimes far more brilliant than me. One of my autistic clients who has successfully built multiple healthy friendships and relationships once said to me, "I can't read social cues, but I can know my own cues." You too may not be able to read all the subtle social cues of neurotypicals, but you can know yourself. If you prioritize and respect yourself, you can have healthy relationships. The following chart will get you thinking about your needs and values as they relate to relationships. This exercise is also available online at http://www.newharbinger.com/53509.

PRIORITIZING YOURSELF IN RELATIONSHIPS

What are your core values?	What are your passions?	What boundaries do you never want violated?
Ex. I believe in treating others as I would prefer being treated and treating everyone with dignity and respect.	I love horror, ghost stories, Star Trek, books, fantasy novels, hiking, backpacking, and running.	I never want to gossip about people or say anything about anyone I haven't said to their face.

What are your core values?	What are your passions?	What boundaries do you never want violated?

Looking at the example in the chart, you can tell a lot about where my boundaries with relationships need to be. I can't be friends with people who gossip. I am not usually good at being friends with people who aren't active because sitting for long periods of time is uncomfortable for me. I can't be friends with people who treat others poorly. Knowing and respecting this will not only keep people I don't want in my life away, but it will also pull the people I do want to me.

So many of us have worked so hard to fit in that we never think who would fit in with *us*. Use the chart above to begin to understand yourself and your needs in relationships. Think about what type of people you might enjoy interacting with and the traits and qualities you want in your relationships. Rather than think of social skills that emphasize you pleasing neurotypicals, think of social skills that emphasize you finding people who make you comfortable and bring you joy because they share your core values, have similar passions, and respect your boundaries.

By knowing and respecting myself, I have sought out activities that I enjoy, and I only engage in them on my timeline. I started an autism support group that meets weekly. In doing this, some of the people I knew casually came and we have built friendships based on mutual respect of each other's burnout cycles and needs as autistic adults. We communicate clearly and don't expect each other to understand our emotional Morse code. I have drawn the people I want into my life by respecting my boundaries.

The Beauty of Being Disliked

Now that you know your needs and values, how do you express your them to others? This can be very challenging. One of the most uncomfortable truths in life is that you will be disliked. Everyone is disliked. Neurotypicals, autistics, and neurodivergent people are all disliked. You can work hard to be perfect, you can mask, and you can say yes to everything that is asked of you and you will still be disliked. You will also be liked. In fact, you will be loved. Some people will love you for your differences and some people who need a safe place to be neurodivergent will find you and like you for who you are.

Who do you know of and respect who is also disliked by some people? This can be a historical figure or celebrity. Why are they disliked?

_____

_____

_____

Being disliked doesn't mean that you are bad or have done anything wrong. People just dislike other people for various reasons. Even among neurotypicals there is dislike over political beliefs, religion, gender, hair color, perspectives. In the book *The Courage to Be Disliked*, Kishimi and Koga hypothesize that people who fear being disliked hate themselves. They fear that who they really are will be seen by others. The courage comes from letting this go and learning to like yourself.

Do you fear being disliked? Describe why you might feel this way.

_____

_____

_____

_____

_____

Accepting that you will be disliked is important because being disliked is inevitable. It is more inevitable because the research shows that neurotypicals will dislike us more than others but also because people are judgmental and prone to disliking each other. It is also important because many autistic people have rejection sensitive dysphoria (RSD), a psychological state that increases your sensitivity and decreases tolerance of rejection, criticism, and taunting. Many autistic people have profound RSD because they were rejected, bullied, and taunted for most of their lives for being different. Failure to meet internal notions of neurotypical expectations can also contribute to their RSD. Most of us struggle with sensory aversions and hypersensitivity in general, which leads to us being more prone to RSD. All of this put together means that many of us become extreme people pleasers as adults. We know we are more disliked than our neurotypical cohorts and yet we have RSD, so we fight desperately to avoid being disliked.

This profound people-pleasing behavior can be one of the most dangerous parts of ASD. This may not make sense on the surface, but if 91 percent of autistic females and 67 percent of autistic males have PTSD, then there must be an explanation that is unique to autism. Lack of social skills and the inability to read people probably plays a significant role, but a profound fear of rejection most certainly increases the probability of being victimized. If we can't be disliked or say no to others—even if forcing ourselves to conform in order to be liked is traumatizing—then abuse and trauma at the hands of other people becomes inevitable.

Furthermore, if we can't be disliked, we will constantly be putting ourselves in situations that decrease our quality of life. Assuming that the double empathy problem won't be resolved in the next few years, we need to be able to have empathy for ourselves even if neurotypicals don't. We need to be able to say no to activities we don't want to do. We need to be able to accept that if we must make ourselves miserable to be liked, then it is better to be disliked. The following exercise will help you examine your fear of rejection and your attempts to be liked. This exercise is also available online at http://www.newharbinger.com/53509.

EXAMINE YOUR FEAR OF BEING DISLIKED

Things you do to make yourself liked that make you uncomfortable.	Would you be more comfortable being disliked or doing the activity?	
Ex. My best friend wanted me to listen to podcasts with her. I have auditory processing disorder and I have never been able to listen to audiobooks and podcasts and maintain focus or understand them. I have to listen several times to digest information I could read once and memorize.	If she can't like me without listening to the podcasts, perhaps she isn't a real friend and I would be more comfortable with her disliking me than listening to something for hours to gain her approval.	
If you are more comfortable being disliked, let go of the activity. It is okay to be disliked. Are you happier not doing the activity?		YES!!

Things you do to make yourself liked that make you uncomfortable.	Would you be more comfortable being disliked or doing the activity?
If you are more comfortable being disliked, let go of the activity. It is okay to be disliked. Are you happier not doing the activity?	
If you are more comfortable being disliked, let go of the activity. It is okay to be disliked. Are you happier not doing the activity?	
If you are more comfortable being disliked, let go of the activity. It is okay to be disliked. Are you happier not doing the activity?	

Now consider what you really gain from seeking to be liked by people versus loving yourself and finding people who love you as you are.

What do you gain from trying to be liked by people who ask you to do uncomfortable things?

_____

_____

_____

_____

_____

You matter. Your comfort and happiness matter as much as anyone else's. Embrace this. Say no. Find the courage to be disliked. You are beautiful just as you are, and you shouldn't have to change who you are just because you are different.

The Outsider in Myths and Stories

One of the most constant and universal archetypal heroes in mythology, literature, folklore, movies, and books is the underdog. The underdog is usually different and shunned by the normal society around them. They must fight to be seen as a valuable part of society and their fight is almost always fierce and fraught with rejection, but the hero triumphs. Everyone loves the underdog.

Think about Harry Potter. He is the boy who lives under the stairs. The Muggles have ostracized him, mocked him, and humiliated him at every turn. He was born different, and he is despised for it. Yet, his difference turns out to be a strength that comes with magic, adventure, and love. He is the hero because of his differences, not despite them. If Harry had fought his differences and rejected his letter to Hogwarts to appease the Muggles, Voldemort would have triumphed and Muggle genocide would have occurred.

In the classic fairy tale *Beauty and the Beast*, Beauty is the youngest daughter of a rich merchant, and she is very different from all her siblings. Her siblings mock her. She is an outsider, but she can save her father because she is so different and she can eventually free the prince from his curse. If Beauty had tried to blend in and act normal, her father would have died in the Beast's prison and the curse never would have been broken.

In the *Odyssey*, Circe is a witch who is condemned to an island because she is different from gods and nymphs alike. She is the daughter of a god and a nymph, and she has never fit in. She eventually acts out, casts some regrettable spells, and is banished to a lonely island. She tries to turn Odysseus's men into pigs, but eventually Circe and Odysseus fall in love. Now she can guide Odysseus to the underworld and help him complete his quest and find his way home. If she had tried to be a nymph or a god and just blended in, Odysseus never would have gotten home.

In *Star Wars*, Luke Skywalker is different from other farmer's sons. He doesn't want to stay on Tatooine and be a farmer. He longs for a different life. He follows Obi-Wan Kenobi on a call to adventure and becomes instrumental in freeing the galaxy from the Galactic Empire.

I could go on and on. All the best stories start with an outsider who doesn't fit in, who longs to be normal and can't be. Through their adventures, they learn that fitting in isn't always the best answer. These stories tell a universal truth that being ordinary isn't necessary and that finding and embracing what makes you unique can save the world.

If you were to write your own outsider myth, what would it be? How would it end? How would the things that make you unique become the key to your journey?

_____

_____

_____

_____

_____

_____

_____

_____

_____

Those of us who are autistic may not save the galaxy or stop curses, but that doesn't mean we can't recognize the beauty that comes with being different and try to find a way to make our uniqueness something that sets us free. The double empathy problem may keep us from ever being fully accepted by all neurotypicals, but it doesn't mean we won't be loved by the ones who count and it doesn't mean that we can't be remarkable. It doesn't mean that how we find beauty in our own stories can't be part of our own folklore.

CHAPTER 6

Autistic Shutdown

You may not be surprised that researchers found out that ongoing social stress could lead to states that almost looked like catatonia in autistic children (Loos and Miller 2004). These states were described as periods of being "dazed, sleepy, and nonresponsive." The states could last for periods ranging from ten minutes to two hours. Since this study, the autistic community has described several distinct states that they feel can occur when we are exposed to too much stress and anxiety. The dazed, sleepy, and nonresponsive state is known as *autistic shutdown*.

The Four Types of Shutdown

The autistic community has created a discourse about how autistic people respond to stress that includes four states. These are burnout, inertia, meltdown, and shutdown (Welch et al. 2020). These four states can be explained as follows:

Autistic burnout is a period of exhaustion experienced by autistic people when they have pushed themselves too hard or when they are overwhelmed. This is usually accompanied by a loss of skills and functionality and increased sensory aversions. This can go on for an extended period of time.

Have you experienced autistic burnout? What things cause you to burn out?

_____

_____

_____

_____

_____

_____

Autistic inertia is the inability of some autistic people to transition from one activity to another. It is hard for us to stop an activity once we are engaged in it and hard for us to start an activity if we aren't engaged in it. Many people interpret this as laziness, but it is not in any way indicative of what would be described as laziness. It can even be an unending train of the same activity that someone appears to be unable to stop.

Have you experienced autistic inertia? What things cause you to enter a state of autistic inertia?

_____

_____

_____

_____

_____

_____

Autistic meltdown is one of the most stereotypical autistic states that is depicted as an autistic child having a "tantrum" at the grocery store or in a public place. This stereotype is dangerous because meltdown is nothing like a tantrum. An autistic meltdown occurs when you have pushed yourself past your capacity to cope. You become completely unable to regulate. This can look like increased stimming, crying, increased echolalia, irrational thoughts, and erratic behaviors. Many of my adult clients describe wanting to die during meltdowns not because death is appealing but because the feelings associated with meltdown are so aversive that they would do anything to make them end. Autistic meltdown is often preceded by periods of burnout that have been ignored.

Have you had autistic meltdowns? If so, what things lead to them?

_____

_____

_____

_____

_____

Autistic shutdown occurs when we push ourselves well past our ability to cope. We may have already burned out or melted down on multiple occasions when this occurs. At this point, our speech and cognitive processing slow. Usually, we seek out quiet places. We can become non-responsive or require excessive prompting to get a response. We may sleep excessively and feel sleepy even when we are well rested.

Have you gone into autistic shutdown? If so, what led to this?

_____

_____

_____

_____

_____

_____

_____

Coping with these four states is the most common thing most autistic people want from autism coaching and therapy. These states can lead to relationship loss, job loss, and massive problems in our interactions with neurotypical society. Since neurotypical society doesn't understand these states, they are usually pathologized and people respond to us like we are broken or "crazy" when we enter into these states. In this chapter, you'll learn some basic techniques to cope with them that can vastly improve your quality of life.

Understanding and Accepting Your Neurological and Physical State

The first step to understanding these rhythms is learning how they apply to you. We are all different. There is no universal type of autism. However, neurologically we do have hyperconnectivity in our brain, which leads us to be more responsive to sensory, social, and cognitive stimuli. We use more of our brain, more of the time, and that is exhausting. Masking and camouflaging behaviors make this emotional exhaustion even more intense. However, the things that will exhaust an individual the most are highly variable.

Many autistic adults have alexithymia, a neuropsychological phenomenon that makes it difficult for us to identify and describe our own emotions or those experienced by others. It also involves social attachment issues and interpersonal relations. For most of us, this means that we often don't understand how we are feeling in the moment. For me it sometimes takes hours or even days for me to fully understand how I am feeling about things. I also rarely realize how upset or burnt out I am until well after I have moved into a place where meltdown is possible. Because it is harder for us to monitor our internal states and we are prone to meltdown, shutdown, and burnout, we have to work harder to prevent these unpleasant things from happening.

The first step to coping with these states is to begin to understand them as they relate to you. I suggest keeping a journal that tracks which stimuli (emotional and physical) create the most stress for you. Imagine you are a scientist, and you are trying to collect data in a study. The following chart is an example you could use as your journal. It is available to download at http://www.newharbinger.com/53509.

Stimuli Date	Loud noises	Social interaction	Time at work	Time in public	Tactile overstimulation	Other:	Other:
Date	Ex. I had to spend time in a loud mall. I noticed significant fatigue.	I went to dinner with friends. Enjoyable but was exhausted after.	I spent 5 hours at work.	I spent 3 hours in a chaotic restaurant.	I had to wear a suit to work. It was itchy and weird.		
Response	Significant fatigue and irritability.	Masking and camouflaging led to decreased mood after.	Exhausted; noticed autistic inertia when changing tasks.	Noticed burnout. Stimming and echolalia significantly increased.	Began to notice signs of shutdown. Didn't respond to people.		

Stimuli	Loud noises	Social interaction	Time at work	Time in public	Tactile overstimulation	Other:	Other:

The goal is to begin tracking the stimuli that are the most exhausting and note which state you are more prone to enter. I am most prone to shutdown. I shut down frequently, and when I do melt down it can be catastrophic, so I try to avoid this at all costs. Besides worksheets like the ones I have created there are numerous apps that allow you to track your mood and activities and monitor how different things impact the way you feel. Breeze is an app that has allowed me to keep track of my mood and has helped me note when I am beginning to move toward shutdown and meltdown.

The following chart shows one way I track my mood and how the environment impacts it. This exercise is also available online at http://www.newharbinger.com/53509.

TRACKING MOOD AND ENVIRONMENT

Day	Mood and State	What Happened	Other Factors
Ex. Monday	Tired and ☹. Back hurts.	I worked 6 hours and someone insulted me.	I went outside more than usual.
Ex. Tuesday	Mood up. Less fatigued.	Saw a friend who hugged me. Worked 4 hours. Painted.	I watched my favorite show.

By tracking your mood and the events that contribute to it you can figure out what is more likely to lead to meltdown or shutdown as well as what helps you recover from these states. By looking at the sample chart above, you can see that a pattern may be forming. Over time, the pattern may become more apparent. You may realize that a daily hug is therapeutic and that the more you work the closer you come to burnout. If you notice enough days with fatigue, pain, and irritability, it is time to add days with activities that you know decrease burnout. By tracking and responding to your internal state with activities that improve your mood, you can decrease the number of times you go into meltdown and burnout.

Coping with Burnout, Meltdowns, and Shutdowns

Sometimes burnout, meltdowns, and shutdowns can't be prevented. Life is challenging and it isn't always possible to keep things calm enough to prevent burnout. Sometimes a meltdown just sneaks up on you and you didn't even realize how bad things were. Sometimes these states just happen. Let's look at Andrew's case.

Andrew's Story

Andrew, a trans man, indicated that his autism wasn't a huge problem for him. He had a supportive partner who was also autistic. His family had taught him not to mask. He had been diagnosed young and gotten the support he needed. However, Andrew struggled with intense periods of panic, anxiety, and crying that often led to suicidal ideation and, on a few occasions, suicide attempts. After discussion, Andrew and I concluded that he was going through regular periods of meltdown, and he became so desperate that he would do anything, including attempting suicide, to make it stop.

Andrew and I spent quite a bit of time talking about these meltdowns. Once they began, he became completely irrational and any attempt to reason with him was futile. However, as we began tracking the meltdowns, we noticed that if he and his partner went into the closet and his partner held him while he rocked back and forth the meltdowns would end sooner and the suicidal ideation would go away.

The more Andrew responded this way to his meltdowns, the fewer meltdowns he had. It was as if just having a plan that helped him cope with the extremeness of the sensation alleviated his anxiety. Andrew began going to his partner before meltdowns and his partner would hold him; this alleviated enough of the pressure that his meltdowns became rare things that only happened in moments of profound stress rather than regular events.

Do you have meltdowns like Andrew? If so, how do they manifest?

_____

_____

_____

Coping skills are complicated because you have to assume that you can't think rationally when you are in these states. Most people who have been through an autistic meltdown describe it as an incredibly irrational place of being completely overwhelmed and trapped in an emotional state you can't escape. There is no rational way out of this, and everyone is different.

For example, when I melt down, I become self-destructive. I rock and cry. I repeat myself. No one can talk to me, but I have melted down enough to know the things that help. If I am with one of my very few safe people, being held tightly helps me a lot. If I am alone, the only thing that can help me is sleeping. Usually if I can get to sleep, I can reboot and feel better when I wake up. Since it is impossible to sleep while I am melting down, I always give myself permission to take two antihistamine tablets. If you have a psychiatrist, you may ask them to prescribe something for meltdowns. Regardless of what your meltdowns look like, it's important to figure out some coping mechanisms.

In the past, what has helped you make it through meltdowns?

_____

_____

_____

_____

Here is a list of things that have helped my clients when they are melting down. Circle any that have worked for you or that you'd like to try.

- Being held

- Going someplace quiet, dark, and alone

- Sleeping

- Losing yourself in a hyperfixation

- Binge-watching a show

- Losing yourself in a glimmer (a sensory delight that soothes you)

- Exercise

- Going someplace different

- Calling a safe person

- Being with a beloved animal

- A weighted blanket

- Medication

- Other:

- Other:

Your go-to coping skill for melting down may not be on this list, but when you are melting down it is okay to do strange things to calm yourself. The only thing you can't do is hurt yourself. If you are prone to self-injury during meltdowns, try to find a substitute that is similar. For example, if you like hitting your head on the wall, try hitting your head on a pillow instead. If you like hitting yourself, try hitting your bed or a stuffed animal.

In the end, the goal is to work toward preventing meltdowns, shutdowns, and burnout and cope well with these states if they happen, but sometimes we can't do this. It is important to be kind to yourself if you have a bad meltdown. Life is hard and it isn't supportive. You should be supportive to yourself.

CHAPTER 7

Communication

Communication is the backbone of human interaction and relationships. It is pivotal to obtaining and maintaining employment, education, pair-bonded relationships, friendships, familial interactions, and even our understanding of ourselves. If communication deficits have impacted you since early childhood, you know that this can be crippling.

The diagnostic criteria for autism are qualitative impairments in reciprocal social interactions, qualitative impairments in communication, and restricted, repetitive, and stereotyped patterns of behavior present since early childhood. So, if you are autistic, you struggle with communication in one form or another. However, this can manifest itself in many ways. Take a moment and look at the chart below. Where are your deficits? What do you struggle with?

How those of us who are autistic struggle with communication is varied. I am hyper-verbal, talking too much. My communication can seem selfish because I can't engage in natural back-and-forth conversation or participate in small talk because I struggle with auditory processing disorder. Some of my clients are almost nonverbal and unable to make eye contact, but are amazing writers who can express themselves with rare beauty when they are allowed to write what they feel. Almost all my clients are unable to understand nonverbal social cues and require direct verbal or written explanations of complex social situations.

As we covered before, most treatments focus on teaching autistic people to communicate like neurotypicals. In this chapter, we are going to take a different direction and focus on finding ways to communicate that keep you safe, reduce your anxiety, and help you better understand the social interactions around you.

Embrace Your Unique Communication Style

The first step is to take a minute and decide how you communicate best. I am best at communicating in writing. I can speak, but I get anxious and talk too much. My auditory processing issues cause me to miss things that are communicated back to me when I am anxious. When I am calm and everything is peaceful, I can communicate very well verbally, but when I am stressed, I send a lot of emails and prefer writing. Here are examples of different communication preferences.

- Lanette is almost entirely nonverbal, but she is able to write beautifully, so she prefers to write notes to people.

- Taylor loves music and sends people song lyrics to explain their feelings.

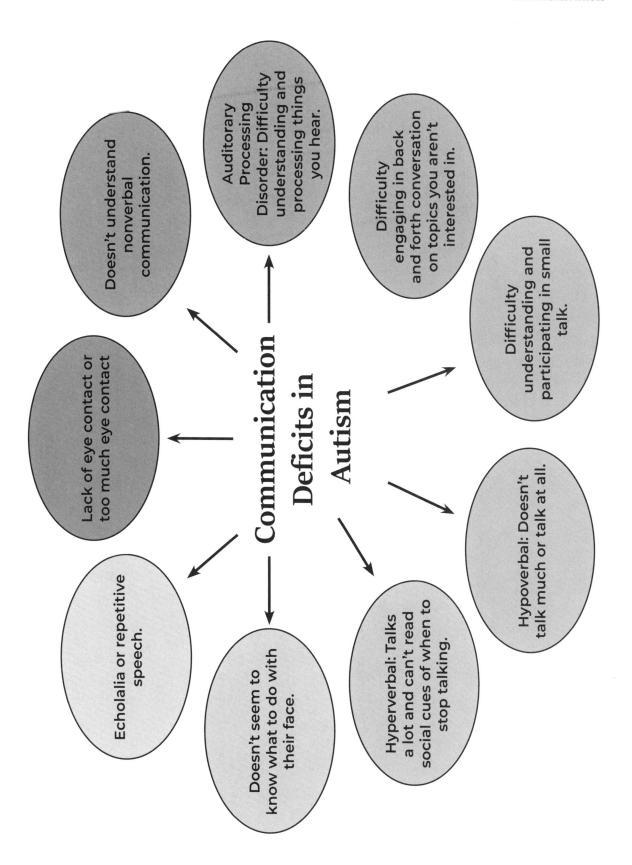

Communication Deficits in Autism

Auditorary Processing Disorder: Difficulty understanding and processing things you hear.

Doesn't understand nonverbal communication.

Lack of eye contact or too much eye contact

Echolalia or repetitive speech.

Doesn't seem to know what to do with their face.

Hyperverbal: Talks a lot and can't read social cues of when to stop talking.

Hypoverbal: Doesn't talk much or talk at all.

Difficulty understanding and participating in small talk.

Difficulty engaging in back and forth conversation on topics you aren't interested in.

- Calson remains quite silent in groups, but he is a leader in the Discord group because his written communication is remarkable when he is texting.

- Barbara just needs extra time to process communication and respond, so she asks for a minute or two to compose a response in her head when she is in a conversation.

Describe how you communicate best. Speaking, writing, slide deck, drawing?

_____

_____

_____

_____

_____

In a perfect world in which your communication style was celebrated, write about how you would communicate with others.

_____

_____

_____

_____

_____

_____

This is what embracing your unique communication style is about—allowing yourself to communicate in a way you feel comfortable with that makes you feel safe and seen. It is okay if this isn't neurotypical or normal. If you must write or text, that is fine. It is also fine if you are too much and if you info-dump or talk about your passions. This is how you connect. Consider how Mark explored communicating after he was diagnosed as autistic.

Mark's Story

Mark was assessed for autism and began treatment with me in the same month. As soon as Mark was diagnosed, he was eager to begin unmasking. He had always struggled fitting in with his family and didn't feel he had ever had any close or meaningful human connections.

After diagnosis, he went to his family and told them he was autistic. He also began to communicate his wants and needs with them directly and bluntly. At work, he did the same. He even began to reach out to old friends and try his new direct communication style with them. He info-dumped freely about his passions and took time to explain his feelings.

Mark lost a few friends and alienated a few family members with his blunt and aggressive style of unmasking, but within a few months he reported having deeper and more meaningful connections with his parents. They told him they had never gotten him before and thought he was being purposefully difficult, but they finally understood him. Several of his friends indicated he seemed more genuine and happier and wanted to spend more time with him.

Mark was only in therapy for a few months. He felt that once he unmasked and started communicating honestly his anxiety and depression dissipated. He felt supported and loved for who he was, not who he was pretending to be. He did mourn the loss of those he had alienated, but the increased closeness with those who mattered made up for the loss.

Set Communication Goals

The next step is to set goals. What do you want to accomplish? It is important that the goals are not about masking or mimicking neurotypical communication styles but about improving your relationships and quality of life. Here are some examples of common neuro-affirmative goals:

- Being able to explain your emotional needs to others

- Improving understanding between yourself and others

- Improving your ability to communicate boundaries

- Improving your ability to state your needs and wants

- Finding a safe person to discuss your hyperfixated interests with

- Improving your ability to communicate at work and social functions

Goals I do not recommend are ones that would continue your masking. These goals would include things like communicating more like a neurotypical, being able to blend in with neurotypicals better, being able to participate in small talk, and being able to participate in neurotypical conversations and social norms. These goals are part of masking and will lead to increased anxiety because they aren't goals you can realistically accomplish without significant distress. Instead, focus on communication that reduces your anxiety and makes you more comfortable.

My communication goals are:

_____

_____

_____

_____

_____

Practice with People Who Feel Safe

It is important to begin practicing communicating in ways that you feel comfortable with, and it helps if you first do this with people you feel safe with. This reduces stress and makes it easier. Some of you may not have a person you feel safe with. That is okay. Trust is a difficult commodity to find. If you do not know someone safe, finding a group may be easier. Many cities have groups for autistic adults and some are better than others. You may want to avoid groups that advertise for help with social skills. If you can't find a good group where you are located, there are a lot of online or Zoom groups you can join. My practice, Tree of Life, offers online groups on Saturday. Autism from the Inside, based out of Australia, also has regular groups. There are groups everywhere. If you can't find safe people, find a safe group.

One of my favorite parts of the autism support group I run is the way we communicate. We don't do small talk. We do not engage in neurotypical back-and-forth conversation. One person says something that matters to them and then another person will tell a story that shows they can relate to the first person's story. People comment on how much they care about the story, but there is no small talk. We take turns info-dumping and asking questions. People close their eyes and avoid eye contact while speaking and listening. People clearly state their needs. They say things like, "Please don't look at me while I talk, it makes me uncomfortable," or "Come back to me; I need to think about what I want to say." We bring special interests and show them off. We talk about physics, Dungeons and Dragons, dogs, crocheting, and all the things that matter to us. We explore communication in a place that is safe and judgment free. Some people in the group prefer remaining mostly silent and only periodically saying something or texting someone. They desire just to be with supportive people. The goal is to explore communication in a safe place and in your own way.

As you begin your journey in working on your communication, pick two or three people you feel the most comfortable with and begin working on communication with them. Write down their names here:

_____

_____

_____

_____

When you find your group or your person or people, explain to them that you are exploring your communication style. This in and of itself is part of practicing expressing yourself. Your first task is to explain your communication needs to them. Let's practice how you might do that.

When you are with your safe person, what information would you like to share? Info-dump as much as you need to.

_____

_____

_____

_____

What stories might you want to share with them?

_____

_____

_____

_____

How will you describe the ways you enjoy communicating the most?

_____

_____

_____

_____

What will you say about your communication styles and needs?

_____

_____

_____

_____

Be Okay Asking Questions

As I previously described, we are bats trying to live as birds. It should go without saying that this will lead to profound difficulties in our ability to communicate with birds. As a bat, you may not be able to read social cues or understand the social world around you. Research has shown that we can't learn to read social cues or understand the complex emotional Morse code of neurotypicals (Park et al. 2016). The only way to fully compensate for these differences is to get comfortable asking for explanations.

I ask questions all the time. It may create anxiety at first, but it helps clarify things in situations where I may not be able to read social cues. For example, I had a recent interaction with an attorney at work. He was smiling and making comments I didn't understand. I asked him to clarify. I asked if he was joking or serious. I asked if it was sarcasm. I explained that he was smiling but the topic seemed quite serious, so I didn't know how to relate to the situation. He clarified and I thanked him. My feelings would have been hurt and I would have perceived him as a bad person if I hadn't taken the time to do this.

I also support this by repeatedly asking others if they have questions and if I made sense. I am aware my communication style is engaging in massive info-dumps and talking about my hyperfixations in ways that may be too niche for neurotypicals who don't share my interests. I am also blunt and have no filter. This can lead to me accidentally hurting people's feelings. By following up and asking if they understood, I allow for people to tell me if I hurt their feelings or went way over their heads and then I can correct and apologize for any unintentional mean things I said. Let's explore how you can feel okay asking questions.

Describe a recent interaction you had when asking questions would have helped.

_____

_____

_____

_____

_____

_____

Identify times when you regularly need to ask questions, such as when you feel someone is angry or when you don't understand what they expect of you.

_____

_____

_____

_____

_____

_____

Write about misunderstandings you have had with neurotypicals that asking and answering questions would help clear up.

_____

_____

_____

_____

_____

_____

Nonverbal Communication

One of the diagnostic criteria for autism is impairment in nonverbal communication. This is defined as lack of eye contact, weak integration between speech and eye contact, body language that neurotypicals perceive as abnormal, and lack of ability to understand other people's body language.

The inability to maintain eye contact is considered the biggest indicator for autism. Research is inconclusive as to what causes this, but my hypothesis has been that it has something to do with the autonomic nervous system and safety cues. Whatever the cause, most autistic people find eye contact extremely aversive, and this is usually the cause of significant criticism throughout our entire lives. For example, Kelly was forced by a teacher to make eye contact while she spoke because it was disrespectful not to. Madison is a very successful engineer. Despite her success and high performance at work, she has been written up three times for being disrespectful in meetings and not making eye contact when spoken to. In the neurotypical world, eye contact seems crucial to how neurotypicals measure respect and whether we are listening.

I have never fully understood the neurotypical obsession with eye contact. I can look at people when they are talking and I can look at people who aren't looking at me, but when I am expected to stare into someone's eyes it feels painful unless it is someone I am intimate with. It feels invasive, like I am trying to peer into someone's soul and they are trying to peer into mine. It feels like I am trying to look at someone naked. Yet, neurotypical society puts a high value on this. I have learned to mask and will force eye contact now, but I have been told that my forced eye contact is often overly aggressive and too much.

When you confront the dilemma of nonverbal communication, the first thing you need to evaluate is how your nonverbal communication impacts you. I have decided that I want to live completely unmasked. I tell everyone I am autistic. I look above the head of the person I am speaking to when I am talking and only make eye contact briefly when they are talking. I stim openly and do not try to interpret neurotypical body language. I just ask questions to try to establish things that could be gathered from body language. This is a choice I made, but you may not be ready to be this open.

Write about eye contact and body language in your environment. How important is it? Have expectations caused you to struggle in school, your career, or with family?

_____

_____

_____

_____

_____

If you said it's not at all important, you could stop here. But if you aren't open about your autism and eye contact matters at work or other places, what is the minimum amount of eye contact you can make and still feel like it won't be a problem?

_____

_____

_____

_____

_____

_____

Can you meet the minimum requirements of your environment without anxiety?

Circle: Yes   No

If the answer is no, you may want to consider altering your environment or unmasking in that environment.

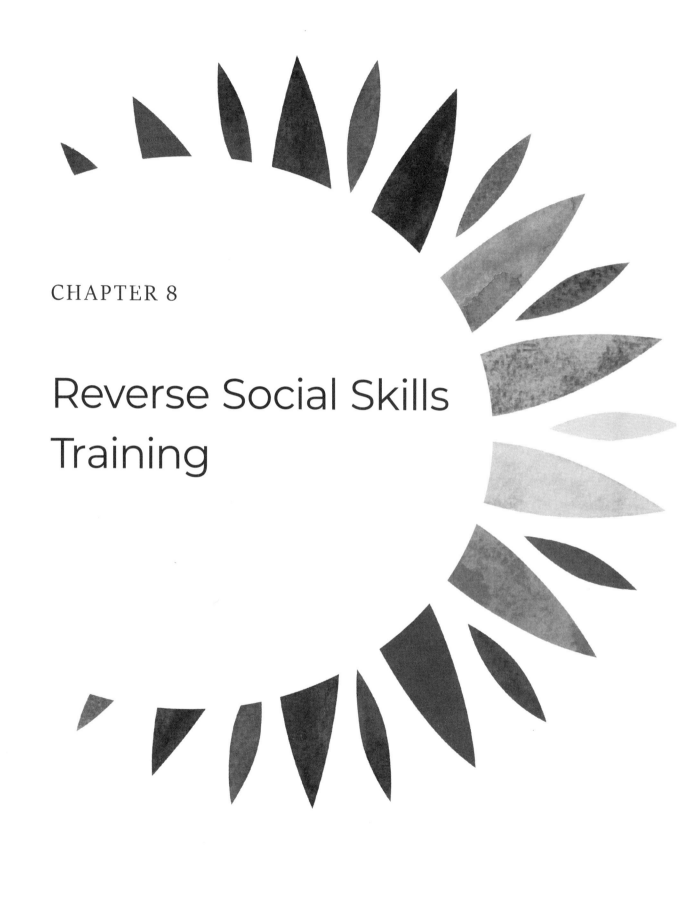

CHAPTER 8

Reverse Social Skills Training

The goal of reverse social skills training is to find that delicate balance between meeting the minimum social skills requirements for your environment and maximizing your comfort and happiness. The goal is to be as unmasked and authentic as you can be in as many situations as possible. Doing this is a personal journey that requires a lot of analysis, so let's start with an analysis of your specific needs. This exercise is also available online at http://www.newharbinger.com/53509.

ANALYZE YOUR SOCIAL SKILLS NEEDS

What places can you safely unmask?	What places do you still need to pretend to be somewhat normal?	What are the minimum skills needed to pretend to be somewhat normal in places that demand masking?
Ex. I unmask almost everywhere.	I still mask at large networking events because being unmasked makes me more anxious than masking.	1. Smile when approached 2. Make minimal eye contact 3. Mind my facial expressions when talking

What places can you safely unmask?	What places do you still need to pretend to be somewhat normal?	What are the minimum skills needed to pretend to be somewhat normal in places that demand masking?

After completing this chart, you should have some idea of the minimum masking that is required of you. The goal is to try to be completely yourself in all other environments. So if you only need to mask at work meetings and when you are in your child's school, then when you are with your family and your partner you should stim, info-dump, and embrace your glimmers to the degree that it gives you joy and provides you peace. This can take many paths that are different from the neurotypical perception of what proper social interaction is. Some people may deeply crave social connections from pair-bonded partners, friends, and family. Others may feel happiest when they are alone and the only real social skill they need is to avoid people staring at them at work. Reverse social skills training is about undoing all neurotypical and societal expectations and spending time focusing on what you need from your interactions with others.

After you look at your minimum masking requirements, describe how much human interaction you have in your life.

_____

_____

_____

_____

_____

Let's dive deeper to help you make clearer decisions about who you interact with. For me, I am quite satisfied with spending much of my free time alone. Before I unmasked, I felt obligated to have a group of friends because I thought that was normal and I was supposed to be normal. I never liked having a group of friends, but I like feeling normal. Once the desire to be normal was removed, I realized I hate being with groups of people. I do like having a pair-bonded partner and have recently gotten married, but I enjoy solitude and the pair-bonded relationship I have. I enjoy my family and have trusted them enough to unmask in front of them. So, I have created an environment in which social skills have largely become just trying to be thoughtful to those I care about. For me, this doesn't mean reading body language or making eye contact, but it means asking how I can best help them and trying to listen when they need to talk about things that cause them anxiety. It also means taking time to learn their wants and needs with clear, verbal communication.

Think about your answer to the last question. If societal expectations were removed, what human interactions do you want? A couple of friends? A pair-bonded partner? A spouse? One friend to go on outings with?

_____

_____

_____

_____

Dealing with Loneliness

Loneliness is one of the largest recurring themes I hear among autistic adults. It is hard for us to meet our social goals. Following is a list of possible places where you could meet neurodivergent people without having to mask.

Autistic adult support groups in your area

Local Dungeons and Dragons groups

Local board game Meetups (Meetup is a site that hosts area clubs and support groups; see www.meetup.com)

Local hiking Meetups

Online autistic adult support groups

Discord servers that support neurodivergent adults

Online role-playing games

The goal is for you to find the connections you need with people who will accept you for who you are. You can always join Tree of Life's online support groups at www.treeoflifebehavioral.com. Follow the link on the website to our Discord server.

Another way to connect with other people is through your hyperfixations, whatever they are. Most autistic people aren't good at small talk and conversation on topics they don't find engaging. However, we can be amazing at talking about things we care deeply about. When you seek out new friends, connect through your hyperfixation interest. This will make conversation easy and eliminate the need for small talk. For example, I am hyperfixated on hiking the Appalachian Trail when I retire. I love hiking and camping. I met my current partner through a hiking Meetup group. We also share a passion for books and both loved *Wheel of Time* and *Dune*. This made conversation easy and facilitated a natural interaction that didn't require masking.

Let Go of Being Liked

Reverse social skills training isn't just about being yourself around the people you want in your life and minimizing masking. As I discussed in chapter 5, it is also about learning to accept that it can be healthy to be disliked. I am going to repeat this.

Sometimes the best thing you can be is disliked.

This can be a hard pill to swallow, but it is the most important social skill you can learn. This social skill will help you be assertive and stand up for yourself and your needs. It will help you set healthy boundaries and protect yourself from abuse and bullying. It will help you unmask and love yourself as you are. If you learn no other social skills but this, learn that you are wonderful even if other people don't like you.

This skill is the opposite of traditional social skills that focus on telling you that you should change your innate behaviors and personality traits to make neurotypicals enjoy your company. But what has the cost of this been on your life? My intense focus on trying to make other people happy and pretending to be normal led to me being abused in my youth, having numerous relationships that collapsed when I could no longer bear the burden of masking, and acute and chronic anxiety and self-hatred. I followed the rules. I used proper social skills as much as I could, but it almost broke me.

What has following the rules of traditional social skills training cost you?

_____

_____

_____

_____

_____

_____

_____

Now go in the other direction. If you let some people dislike you, how could it improve your life? For me, being my weird, true self has pushed many people out of my life and I am disliked by a lot of people, but it has made me closer to some old friends who see me as a safe shore for their atypical selves. I am now a safe haven for all the tattooed, anime-loving, role-playing, rainbow-colored hair, LGBTQIA+, neurodivergent people in my area, and all of that was built on the fact that I just let myself be my own natural weird self. Having the courage to be disliked has allowed me to say no to several people who were trying to take advantage of me and push people out of my life who were hurting me. It has allowed me to set boundaries around my time so I get the alone time I need and can live the life I need to be the best version of myself I can be.

What could you gain if you just let yourself be disliked?

_____

_____

_____

_____

_____

_____

Trauma Prevention

The vast majority of autistic adults have a history of trauma. Abandoning the need to be liked and letting go of traditional social skills is critical because the most important social skill you can be taught is to prioritize your safety and well-being above all else. You never need to set yourself on fire to keep anyone warm, and you should never sacrifice yourself to please others. You are autistic. You are not bad. You are not unworthy of care or love. You deserve to be treated with the same loving kindness as everyone else, and if the people in your life can't do that, you may need new people in your life.

This is the most important social skill most of us need to learn: to avoid people who will hurt you and set boundaries around people in your life, so you won't be hurt. This is an incredibly complex process as most of us can't read social cues and this includes cues of danger and safety.

Here is a list of red flags you can look for to help identify unsafe or unhealthy people:

1. They "love bomb" you, or act too affectionate and loving too fast before they have had time to get to know you.

2. They use condescending language.

3. They regularly cross your boundaries or ask you to do things you aren't comfortable with.

4. They isolate you from friends or family.

5. They say things to you that make you feel bad.

6. They put their needs consistently above yours.

7. They have a history of abusing others.

8. They have an explosive temper and erratic moods.

9. They are unwilling to compromise or respect your needs.

10. They are an active abuser of drugs or alcohol.

On the flip side, it is also important to look for green flags in a relationship. Here is a list of green flags you can look for to help identify safe and healthy people:

1. They respect your boundaries and listen to you.

2. They work to communicate with you in a way you can understand.

3. They are kind to you and value your needs and wants.

4. You feel safe with them.

5. They don't judge you and you feel comfortable unmasking around them.

6. They are willing to compromise.

7. They set their own healthy boundaries around their needs.

8. They are honest.

9. They can have a disagreement and still treat you with respect.

10. They never pressure you to do things you are uncomfortable doing.

Have you ever been in a situation with people who might hurt you and you didn't notice or realize it? Describe the situation.

_____

_____

_____

_____

_____

_____

_____

_____

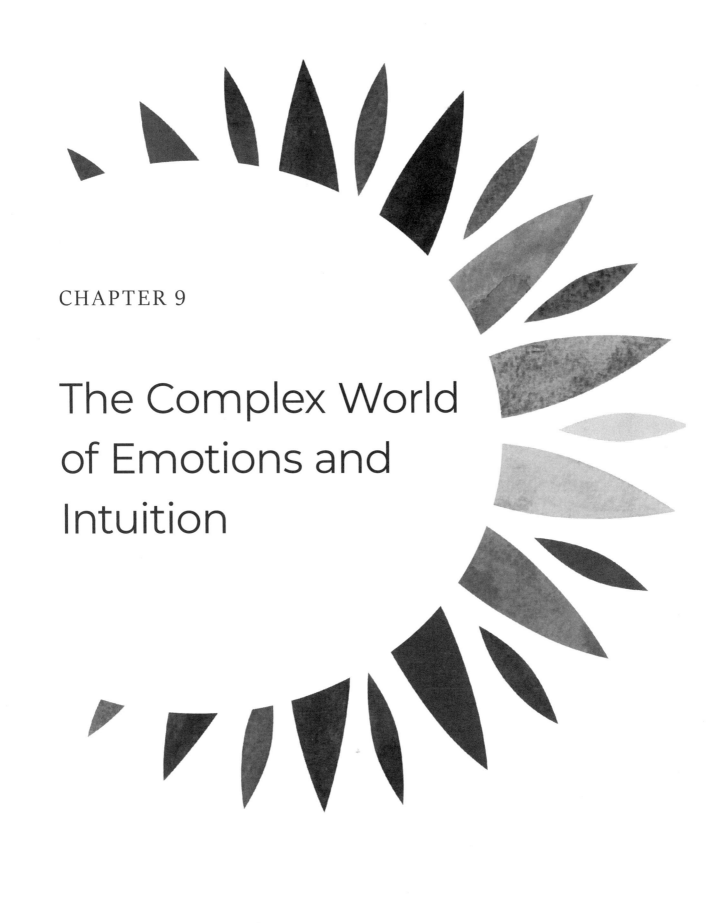

CHAPTER 9

The Complex World of Emotions and Intuition

Have you ever had someone ask you how you feel, and you haven't had an answer? Have you ever had someone ask you what is going on with you and you genuinely don't know? Most neurotypicals don't understand this. It is incomprehensible to them, but this is very common for autistic people. We commonly don't know how we feel. What can make this more frustrating is that common techniques for pain and mood identification just don't work for us.

Alexithymia is the word that describes this difficulty processing and understanding your own emotions and bodily states. New research has shown that alexithymia, one of the more common features of autism spectrum disorder, is the key factor that regulates autistic people's difficulties knowing what to do with their face and their voice (Oakley et al. 2022). Not all autistic people have alexithymia, but many do (Kinnaird, Stewart, and Tchanturia 2019).

Current research is driven toward understanding what causes alexithymia. Neuroimaging studies comparing different levels of autism and physiological studies looking at skin conductance are making progress into explaining why many autistic people can't understand their own internal states. This is brilliant, but somehow it fails to explain how difficult it is to live with alexithymia. In "decoupling" models of alexithymia, the physiological arousal induced by an emotional state is not integrated with conscious awareness of this arousal. This could represent a key shared mechanism between autism and alexithymia, reflecting research that suggests there is a disruption between how autistic people subjectively experience their emotions and their physiological emotional arousal.

Living with Alexithymia

When I was in my forties, I didn't realize how entirely disconnected I was from myself until I was diagnosed as autistic. If you had asked me if I was an anxious person I would have said no. But anxiety in dozens of situations drove my behavior and led to multiple autistic burnout, meltdown, and shutdown states throughout my life. Everyone who has known me would have described me as anxious—except me. At every doctor's appointment I have been to, I describe my pain levels as 5 because I don't understand the difference between pain from a stubbed toe versus a broken bone. When I had my first son, it took forty-eight hours for me to deliver because I didn't understand the concept of pushing. I struggle to identify when I am sad unless I am actively bottoming out. I do know when I am happy and elated. I can feel that, but other emotions are elusive.

This has led to a coping skill that most of my autistic clients also engage in. Since we can't feel things, we try to reason through them. I can't comprehend fear, so I try to look around and see things in my environment that should be scary and analyze their risk based on several reasonable constructs. I can't feel pain properly, so I try to logic my way through whether it is reasonable to be distressed by the severity of a situation. This is time-consuming and exhausting, and I am often very wrong. I will end up in the ER for a stubbed toe and will ignore a broken bone. I will run happily into dangerous situations and avoid safe ones. Gut instincts are critical in decision making, and I have none. This has been particularly crippling in pair-bonded relationships. I have read dozens of books and articles on what makes a happy relationship to figure out the algorithm that is love. But love is not an algorithm. It is something you feel. So what does that mean if you can't identify what you feel?

Let's start with a basic exercise. Just sit in a comfortable spot and try to be in the present moment. Let go of reason and logic. Let go of thinking. Thoughts will come and thoughts will go. Focus on the moment. In this moment, focus on your breathing.

Scan your body one area at a time. Notice the temperature, such as cold, cool, lukewarm, or hot. Notice other sensations, such as tense, soft, or sore.

How do your feet feel? _____

How do your hands feel? _____

How do your legs feel? _____

How do your arms feel? _____

How does your back feel? _____

How does your face feel? _____

What is your breathing like? (e.g., rapid, gentle, difficult? _____

What is your heartbeat like? (e.g., slow, fast?) _____

Overall, how does your body feel? (e.g., tense, relaxed, flushed?) _____

What is your mood like? Any word will do. (e.g., purple, pink, happy, sad, blank, euphoric, angry, irritated, stupid, tired?) _____

How hard was it for you to do this exercise? Did you shut down when we got to mood or were you able to pick a word? Was the word different from something most people would choose for a mood?

_____

_____

_____

Some autistic people relate to emotions in different ways than neurotypicals. Olivia referred to how they felt about others in colors. They also had colors to describe their emotions. After a while, we were able to figure out what the colors meant. We were able to learn that safe people were green and dangerous people were red. Purple people were too much and led to sensory overload. We charted their emotions using their words and were able to come up with a strategy for recognizing their feelings and coping with them.

Identifying Your Emotions

According to research, being able to understand your emotions is critical to positive outcomes and better quality of life for autistic people (Oakley et al. 2022). Understanding your emotions is also critical to preventing burnout and meltdown states. Some of us are like blind people: the world of emotion is there for us and it impacts us, but since we can't see it, we don't know how to navigate and end up getting hurt more than most. Some autistic people can interpret their emotions if they are given enough time (Oakley et al. 2022). Let's look at your emotional life to work on identifying emotions.

Do you remember when in your life you were happiest? If so, write down the memory.

_____

_____

When were you happy recently? Describe the situation.

_____

_____

What did being happy feel like in your body?

_____

_____

Do you remember when in your life you were saddest? If so, write down the memory.

_____

_____

When were you sad recently? Describe the situation.

_____

_____

What did sadness feel like in your body?

_____

_____

Do you remember when in your life you were angriest? If so, write down the memory.

_____

_____

When were you angry recently? Describe the situation.

_____

_____

What did anger feel like in your body?

_____

_____

Do you remember when in your life you were the most anxious? If so, write down the memory.

_____

_____

When were you anxious recently? Describe the situation.

_____

_____

What did anxiety feel like in your body?

_____

_____

Do you remember when in your life you were most excited? If so, write down the memory.

_____

_____

When were you excited recently? Describe the situation.

_____

_____

What did excitement feel like in your body?

_____

_____

Are you noticing any patterns in your emotions? Any identifiable features? Recognizing your emotions is important, and listening to those emotions is even more important. Many autistic people have been taught to suppress their emotions. They were taught to eat foods that created anxiety and panic and go places that put them into sensory overload and caused terror. This is part of what teaches us to ignore our emotions.

Think back to your childhood. When were you taught to ignore your emotions? How did it impact how you relate to your emotions now?

_____

_____

_____

_____

Making Decisions

Alexithymia can impact your life in almost every way. Neuroscientist Antonio Damasio discusses how important emotion is to functioning in his book *Descartes' Error* (2005). In it, he discusses a man he calls Elliot who got a brain tumor in the frontal lobe of his brain. The tumor was removed but his life fell apart after removal. He wasn't able to make basic decisions and this led to him losing his job. He was unable to complete projects. He got divorced. He was still intelligent and had a good memory, but his life was a mess. IQ tests showed no deficits. What Damasio discovered following significant testing was that Elliot's ability to feel and understand emotion was completely impaired. Damasio's research shows that we need our emotions to make basic decisions. It isn't our logical mind that makes us decisive and capable, it is the delicate balance between reason and emotion.

If you have alexithymia, this is likely why you struggle to accomplish tasks. It could be hypothesized that some of the serious executive functioning issues associated with autism could at least be in part contributed to alexithymia.

So how do we fix this problem? The answer is to track and acknowledge your feelings on a daily basis, and then listen to your feelings. Try to identify how you feel about things and make decisions based not just on logic, but also on emotion. The following exercise will help you log your daily feelings. This exercise is also available online at http://www.newharbinger .com/53509.

__/__/___

S M T W TH F S

An Autistic Survival Guide
to

Tracking Your Feelings

Breathe First

INHALE EXHALE INHALE EXHALE INHALE EXHALE

Things that caused tension

* _____
* _____
* _____
* _____
*

Describe my feeling in a Drawing

Things that overwhelmed me

Today I feel:

Things that brought joy:

_____
_____
_____
_____

Am I moving towards or away from burnout today?

_____
_____

AUTISTIC SURVIAL
TOOLS

By tracking your feelings daily, you can begin to get an idea of how your feelings impact you and how you respond to stressors. It can also help you prevent burnout and meltdown by giving you a road map to understand what feelings mean to you and how they relate to your burnout and meltdown phases. John's story shows how vital this process is.

John's Story

In high school John thought he had multiple friends. In retrospect, he now knows that this group of boys was bullying him. They called him names and periodically even hit him. He followed them and they used him as the butt of their jokes. Sometimes they stole his things and hid them from him. In our discussion, he indicated that he knew these boys were making him uncomfortable, but he didn't know how uncomfortable, so he didn't know to tell them to stop. He struggled with alexithymia and this led to him continuing to hang out with boys who were actively hurting him. His mother saw what was happening and advocated on his behalf. The bullying stopped, but John still did not understand that these boys weren't his friends. In fact, he invited them to his birthday party.

John worked through the complex emotions he had and the trauma associated with the bullying. Setting boundaries continued to be a problem for him in adulthood, and he had dated women who had taken advantage of him. To identity his inner cues, he started identifying when he was uncomfortable. He noted what he felt in his body as well as the emotions associated with them. Then he began telling others when he was uncomfortable and setting boundaries around that discomfort. This led to healthier relationships.

Intuition and Gut Instincts

In the neurotypical world, it is common knowledge that much of life isn't about reason but rather about "listening to your intuition" and "following your heart." Neurotypicals talk a lot about these things. They give advice that says, "Follow your gut instinct."

All these things are code for listening to your autonomic nervous system. Your autonomic nervous system is a branch of your peripheral nervous system that regulates your fight-or-flight response. Your autonomic nervous system is divided into three parts. The first part is the sympathetic nervous system. This activates when you perceive danger. Danger can be environmental or interpersonal. Our sympathetic nervous system is wired for us to sense danger in a person's tone of voice, body language, and facial expressions. All higher-level vertebrates have this. If you watch dogs, you can see it working. Dogs approach new dogs slowly, watching every subtle gesture for cues of danger. The sympathetic nervous system is also designed to activate when there are environmental dangers like fire, predators, or storms.

The second part of the autonomic nervous system is the parasympathetic nervous system. It is divided into two parts: the ventral vagal parasympathetic nervous system and the dorsal vagal parasympathetic nervous system. The ventral vagal system regulates cues of safety and helps higher vertebrates interpret social cues. The dorsal vagal system regulates the shutdown, freeze, and dissociative parts of the autonomic nervous system. This is activated in cases of extreme danger.

Research by Stephen Porges has shown that there is significant dysregulation of the autonomic nervous system in autistic people. In a 2019 article for *Spectrum News*, Dr. Porges said that the brain-body connection may ease autistic people's social problems. He said, "My research has documented parallels between the autonomic system—the system that controls the fight-or-flight system and the functioning of our organs—and difficulties with learning and socializing. Essentially, if we cannot regulate our physiological state, we cannot socialize and connect with others."

This explains many of our struggles. It also partially explains alexithymia and our inability to read social and safety cues. Long story short, most autistic people have no "gut instincts." This often leads to us trying to reason our way through situations that require a "gut" or instinctual response. The reason vertebrates have an autonomic nervous system is because it isn't in our best interest to stop and reason our way through life-and-death situations. When a tiger attacks, we need to act without thought. The response needs to be fluid. When we meet new people, we need to just be able to read danger and safety cues and not do a twenty-minute mental analysis of everything we know about their history to determine whether they are safe.

This lack of gut instinct leaves you vulnerable. Reason cannot always interpret cues of safety and danger. As I said in chapter 5, 91 percent of autistic women and 67 percent of autistic people in general also meet diagnostic criteria for PTSD. That means that we are frequently preyed on by dangerous people. We enter abusive relationships because we can't tell whether someone is dangerous. We go dangerous places because we can't read safety cues. We are assaulted, abused, bullied, and hurt because we lack the ability to perceive threats accurately. We are blind to cues that are intuitive to neurotypicals with no trauma history. Jane's story illustrates this.

Jane's Story

Jane had never dated when she left for college. In high school and middle school, she had a social network that centered on her hyperfixated interest in dance. In school, her entire life had been dance. Largely because of this, no one thought she was autistic. She always had activities and friends because she went to dance four days a week and studied the rest of the time. She was smart and her family sheltered her. Her family reported later that they knew she was weird when she was young and tried to teach her to be more normal so people would like her. This led to Jane masking a lot to cover her autistic traits.

In college, Jane began dating an older man. She didn't have any friends and didn't know how to make friends. Since she wasn't in dance, her natural social group was gone. Her roommate warned her the man she was dating was bad news, but Jane took everything the man said literally and at face value. He made her promises and told her he loved her, and she trusted all of this explicitly. Even after John assaulted her and abused her on numerous occasions, Jane failed to understand the severity of the situation. In retrospect, she blamed herself for being so stupid. She asked herself how anyone could be dumb enough to miss all the danger cues that appeared in the early stages of the relationship.

Once she was able to identify the situations that were hurting her, she could set boundaries around herself and her safety, and later leave the relationship. She continues to work on her alexithymia, safety and danger cues, and working through her trauma.

Have you ever felt you missed cues of safety and danger that neurotypicals can perceive? If so, what happened?

_____

_____

_____

_____

How do you think this has impacted your life?

_____

_____

_____

_____

_____

Do you have a trauma history that has been shaped by your inability to read safety and danger cues? Write about how these experiences might be connected.

_____

_____

_____

_____

_____

_____

How would it have helped you to have a better gut instinct? What might have happened differently?

_____

_____

_____

_____

_____

_____

Have you been in unhealthy relationships or had unhealthy friendships because of your inability to determine whether people are safe? Describe some of them.

_____

_____

_____

_____

_____

_____

Dealing with Trauma

If you have trauma and autism, then you have struggled with human interactions in ways most people will never understand or relate to. Being autistic can feel like you have been released in a forest filled with wolves and you have no sense of sight. You are wandering blindly trying to find some safe places. This is terrifying and can lead to a lot of hurt. If this is your story, you will need treatment for your trauma as well as help navigating being autistic.

There are many treatments for trauma. Eye movement desensitization and reprocessing (EMDR), narrative therapy, cognitive behavioral therapy, internal family systems therapy (IFS), and somatic therapies can all help you move through your trauma. This is the moment when a workbook won't be enough. I encourage you to find a neuro-affirmative therapist who is familiar with trauma and autism and can help guide you through the process of healing.

Even if you don't have full-blown PTSD, your inability to read safety, social, and danger cues has probably led to a lot of anxiety and stress. Using reason isn't as helpful as it should be, and we can't learn to regulate our autonomic nervous system, but we can learn coping skills to deal with our distress. Things that I have found helpful include somatic therapies such as yoga and Reiki. Mindfulness-based therapies are also helpful. (Exercises based on these approaches can be found in the supplemental materials at www.treeoflifebehavioral. com.) You can also explore the Safe and Sound Protocol designed by Dr. Stephen Porges and other polyvagal-based approaches. These things should also be explored with a therapist.

However, one thing that can help you with safety is learning to listen to your discomfort and respond to it by setting healthy boundaries. Many of us were trained to ignore our own discomfort. For example, we were taught to eat foods we found aversive and push through sensory overwhelm. This has taught us not to listen to our bodies. This skill can be helpful as some ability to cope with discomfort is necessary, but it can be toxic when you learn to tune out things that are dangerous. For example, many autistic people can't tell between a 1 and a 10 on a pain/discomfort scale, and eating broccoli versus being abused can register as the same level of discomfort for us. So, the goal is to start by listening to your discomfort and responding to it. You may not have strong cues of safety and danger, but you can learn to respect the cues you do know and recognize. This will help keep you safe, and your safety matters.

When was the last time you felt uncomfortable?

_____

_____

_____

How did you respond to that discomfort? Did you respect your own needs and boundaries? If not, how could you have respected your needs?

_____

_____

_____

_____

_____

_____

_____

_____

When was the last time a person made you uncomfortable? How did you respond to that?

_____

_____

_____

_____

_____

How could you respond to that in the future, in a way that respects your boundaries and keeps you safe?

_____

_____

_____

_____

_____

Remember that the goal of this book isn't to teach you how to make other people happy but rather to give you an improved quality of life. Part of that is learning to set and communicate strong boundaries and be assertive so that you are safe and surrounded by people who will keep you safe. This may mean you have fewer friends and social interactions, but better to have one safe friend than a dozen friends and relationships that damage you and cause you trauma.

Distress Tolerance

One of the most important parts of understanding your emotions is learning to cope with them. Once you have spent time sitting with your emotions and can begin to understand them, it is time to practice what to do with them. Distress tolerance is the ability to cope with emotions without feeling overwhelmed by them. Because autistic people struggle with understanding emotions, we often become overwhelmed by them.

Many autistic people either over- or underreact to situations that are uncomfortable. Bright lights at the mall can lead to complete meltdowns, whereas abusive situations can lead to calm. Now that you have begun to recognize and understand when you should react, the question is how to react and how to modulate that. For many of us, the best way to do this is with planning and with mindfulness.

Let's start with a simple exercise. The next time you realize you are anxious or uncomfortable, stop and do this activity after you ensure that you are safe. Remember, all emotions are temporary. Your goal is to make it through an uncomfortable moment.

Take five deep breaths. Just breathe naturally. Don't change your breath. Just count out each breath. Now take three more breaths. Make the exhale longer than the inhale. Count the duration of your inhale. Breathe in for four seconds and out for eight seconds. Now look around. Label the things you see. Allow yourself to observe the uncomfortable emotion. Don't make decisions or try to run from it. Just observe it and ask yourself: *Am I having a meltdown?* If yes, follow your meltdown plan.

My meltdown plan: _____

_____

Next, ask yourself: *Am I reacting to a life event or a situation I can control?* If you can change the situation, change it. If not, follow your meltdown plan to comfort yourself and try to focus on the things you can control. For example, if the temperature is uncomfortable, change the thermostat. If you are thirsty, get a drink. Take control of what you can around you and accept that sometimes anxiety and sadness are natural and normal. This is a hard concept, but when our body is injured, pain is its way of telling us to stop doing what we are doing. Our emotions are no different.

Things I can control: _____

_____

Next, allow yourself to feel the uncomfortable emotions and listen to them. What are your emotions telling you might help? Make a list of things that help you when you are upset, such as calling a friend, going for a walk or run, following your meltdown plan, going to your sensory bag, or petting an animal. Allow yourself to take time to comfort yourself through the uncomfortable emotion.

Things that help when I'm upset: _____

_____

Sometimes simple plans don't work, and uncomfortable emotions and distress can be so overwhelming they can consume us. They can turn into depression, generalized anxiety, or panic. Most autistic people have at least one depressive episode and have experienced generalized anxiety at some point in their lives. If simple activities like mindfulness and self-soothing don't work, it is always best to seek professional help. You don't have to face this alone.

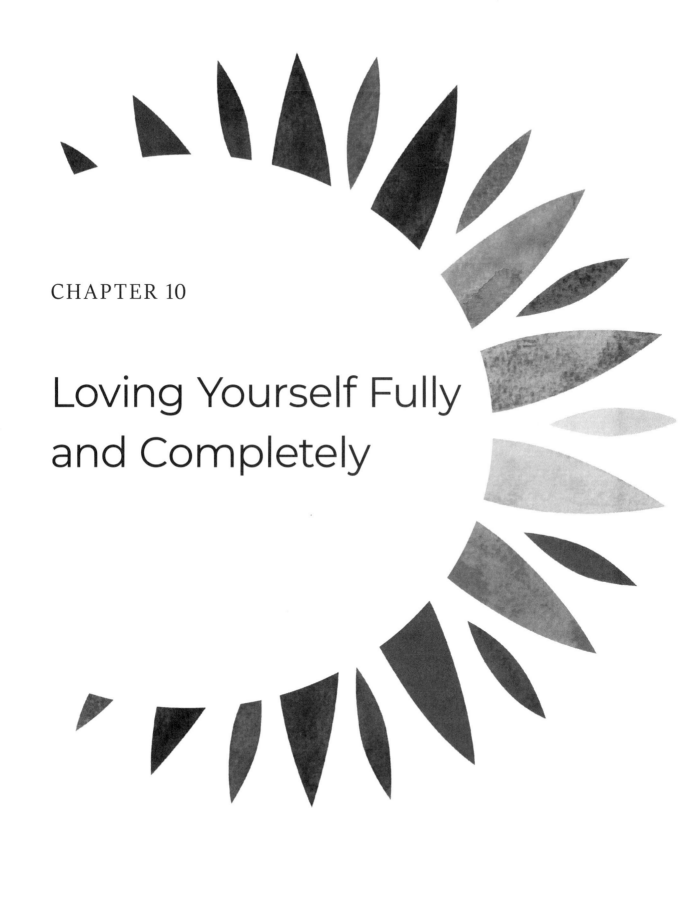

CHAPTER 10

Loving Yourself Fully and Completely

In *NeuroTribes*, Steve Silberman writes, "It seems that for success in science and art, a dash of autism is essential. For success, the necessary ingredient may be an ability to turn away from the everyday world, from the simply practical, an ability to rethink a subject with originality to create in new untrodden ways."

The world has spent so much time pathologizing autism that it is hard to see the beauty in it. Sometimes when you are autistic it is hard to see the beauty in yourself. If you have spent your life melting down, being bullied, losing jobs, struggling in school, or being rejected, it is hard to wake up and celebrate your autism. However, it is important to begin seeing the possibilities in your autism—that the problem isn't with you but with a society that values conformity above novelty. You have beauty and infinite possibility locked up within you.

I love my autism support group. Every time I go to it, I see the possibilities within autism. Everyone there has struggled. Everyone there has wanted to be normal at times in their life. However, when I listen to group members info-dump about physics, or teas, or Dungeons and Dragons, or the history of the Kennedy family, I know that there must be something more powerful in the language of autism. There's more than the neurotypical act of losing yourself in to-and-fro conversations about the mundane clockwork of daily life. In autistic language, novel ideas and ways of perceiving the world are nurtured and grown. There is a brilliance in that room that is born out of the uncommon beauty of every autistic person, and I deeply believe the future is neurodivergent.

Autistic Role Models

The list of remarkable people in this world contains innumerable autistic individuals, including people who have changed the world. Some of these people have official medical diagnoses and some we can conclude were autistic based on behavioral data. Either way, the goal of this book and the goal of autism treatment is to help you learn to cope with the hard parts of autism while beginning to embrace who you are. You are remarkable, and you should welcome this.

As you begin to work on loving yourself as you are, it can help to have autistic role models. My autistic role models include Emperor Claudius, Hermione Granger, Jane Eyre, and Carl Jung. You may notice some of my autistic role models are fictitious. This is important because whether they know it or not, the neurotypical world has a place for people who are autistic, and when they create fictional worlds, they always put us in them. Having fictional and real autistic role models reminds us that neurotypicals need and want us in their best versions of life.

Who are your autistic role models?

_____

_____

_____

_____

_____

What do you admire about your role models?

_____

_____

_____

_____

_____

_____

What autistic traits make your role models remarkable?

_____

_____

_____

_____

_____

How did (or does) the neurotypical world react to your role models?

_____

_____

_____

_____

_____

What can you learn from your autistic role models?

_____

_____

_____

_____

_____

Finding Your Tribe

One of the most difficult parts of living as autistic is feeling like an outsider. It is hard for us to find that human connection that neurotypicals take for granted. So where do we begin? The first step is to chase your hyperfixated interests. If you love Dungeons and Dragons, go to your local gaming store and find groups that play. If you love chess, join a chess league. If you love a video game, join a Discord group online. Chase your passions. Embrace them fully. Find people who love them as much as you do.

My interest: _____

Groups based on my interest: _____

_____

My interest: _____   _____

Groups based on my interest: _____

_____

My interest: _____

Groups based on my interest: _____

_____

One of the beautiful things about this moment in the history of autism is that social groups are popping up everywhere for autistic adults, and so are support groups. In the small city I live in, we have two Meetup groups for autistic adults. We also have a group called Weird Kids for Life that has a lot of autistic adult members. Seek out the weird autistic people in your area to find your tribe.

Do some research into local groups. Write down their names and meeting times. Then plan to go!

_____

_____

_____

Human connection is important for all of us, and you don't have to be alone. If you can't find people where you live, find people online. There are many of us out here.

Some online groups I am interested in attending include:

_____

_____

_____

Self-Advocacy and Coming Out as Autistic

Unmasking and coming out as autistic are two different things. You can be yourself and let your autistic traits manifest without telling everyone you are autistic. This is a conversation we have a lot in my support group. Should you come out as autistic? Should you tell your family, friends, and coworkers? This is a deeply personal decision, as everyone has unique lives and different variables. For example, when I came out as autistic, I was terrified it would destroy my career. Who wants an autistic therapist? Until I came out, I hid my tattoos in session and was careful to act neurotypical around my clients. Despite this, when I came out, it actually helped my career. My family supported me passionately because it explained so much of my behavior and it helped some of my other family members in their lives.

However, other people have jobs where they are discriminated against when they come out as autistic. They are fired or driven out. Some employers don't want employees they will have to give special treatment to. If you have a job like this, coming out as autistic can be devastating. Similarly, some people have families and friends that they know will be safe and supportive; others have families and friends that hold old beliefs about autism and do not embrace mental health.

Coming out as autistic is deeply personal. It is a decision you alone can make. You can use the following exercise to help you decide. This exercise is also available online at http://www .newharbinger.com/53509.

RISKS AND BENEFITS OF COMING OUT AS AUTISTIC

Where am I considering coming out as autistic?	What benefits would I get from coming out as autistic?	What is the likelihood they will accept me on a scale of 1 (accepting) to 10 (highly judgmental)?	Based on this chart, do the benefits outweigh the risks?
Ex. My child's school	People would know why I avoid PTO and crowded events and not judge my child for my atypical behavior.	In all likelihood the women at my child's school would not be accepting, so I give this an 8. They tend to be judgmental and harsh.	Risks are higher. I will not tell people.

Where am I considering coming out as autistic?	What benefits would I get from coming out as autistic?	What is the likelihood they will accept me on a scale of 1 (accepting) to 10 (highly judgmental)?	Based on this chart, do the benefits outweigh the risks?
Ex. Work	People at work would understand why I am not always social and know I don't mean to be rude.	I am a therapist and my work environment is supportive, so the likelihood of being accepted is a 1.	Risks are low and acceptance is high. I will tell people at work.

Things you may also want to consider are: Do you want an official diagnosis? Do you want this on your medical record? Do you want this in legal documents? Do you need or want disability services?

As you consider these things, be aware that the more you come out, the more you will have to advocate on your own behalf. You will have to face people who say things like, "You don't seem autistic to me," and you will need to have scripts for dealing with people like this. My script for dealing with this is carrying a highlighted copy of Sarah Hendrickx's book *Women and Girls with Autism Spectrum Disorder.* I hand people my favorite highlighted page. It says, "Even now, my greatest fear, source of indignation, and sadness is the disbelief of others. I have not worked out how to respond politely to someone I met only a few minutes ago who tells me, with apparent great authority, that I am not autistic, when every part of my inner being wants to say, 'And how the **** do you know?' And cry."

For some reason, this tends to stop people in their tracks. Even doctorate-level psychologists tend to stop questioning. However, this script may not work for you. My go-to script when I don't have my book is info-dumping about the history of autism. I think I bore them away. What scripts might work for you?

My first plan for when people say I don't seem autistic:

_____

_____

_____

_____

_____

My second plan for when people say I don't seem autistic:

_____

_____

_____

_____

_____

I enjoy self-advocacy because I love talking about autism. It is my hyperfixation and these moments give me a chance to info-dump on people about autism. For those of you who don't enjoy this, you may have to be more careful in your decisions. The goal is to make your unique needs the priority and know that all autistic adults have different needs. Embrace your needs and make choices that will bring you the most happiness and the best quality of life.

Loving Yourself

If you take one thing from this workbook, it should be that you are beautiful just as you are. We all periodically need self-improvement that moves us toward being happier and healthier, but who you are at your core should be something you seek to find, cherish, and celebrate, not something you should hide or run from. Autistic people are some of the most magnificent, beautiful people in the world and being basic shouldn't be celebrated. You should be you.

The poet E. E. Cummings wrote, "The hardest challenge is to be yourself in a world where everyone is trying to make you someone else." This is profoundly true for those of us who are autistic. Around us, every day, there are people telling us to live life by their rules. But who decided those rules? Why are they better? Do they work for everyone? They don't, and the goal of this workbook is to help you embrace that at the deepest level.

Therefore, find a way to live by your own rules. Find a way to thrive by building a life that works for you even if the neurotypicals think it is strange or wrong. Every day, wake up and look for your autistic strengths. Look for the beauty in your uniqueness. Don't put other people's expectations on yourself. Listen to your own wants and needs. Live deliberately for yourself and prioritize your happiness.

We are weird, and that is a magic unto itself.

Acknowledgments

Thank you to Rainn Stone, LMSW. Your contributions to my research and to building a support network out of Tree of Life have been invaluable. Your vision and support have made my work possible.

References

Alkhaldi, R. S., E. Sheppard, E. Burdett, and P. Mitchell. 2021. "Do Neurotypical People Like or Dislike Autistic People?" *Autism Adulthood* 3(3): 275–279.

American Psychiatric Association. *Diagnostic and Statistical Manual of Mental Disorders (DSM).* 2013. Washington, DC: American Psychiatric Publications.

———. *Diagnostic and Statistical Manual of Mental Disorders, 5th Edition, Text Revision (DSM-5-TR).* 2022. Washington, DC: American Psychiatric Publications.

Bettelheim, B. 1967. *The Empty Fortress: Infantile Autism and the Birth of the Self.* New York: Free Press.

Broderick, A. A. 2022. *The Autism Industrial Complex: How Branding, Marketing, and Capital Investment Turned Autism into Big Business.* Gorham, ME: Myers Education Press.

Cannon, J. 2007. *Stellaluna.* New York: Clarion Books.

Cassidy, S., L. Bradley, R. Shaw, and S. Baron-Cohen. 2018. "Risk Markers for Suicidality in Autistic Adults." *Molecular Autism* 9: 42.

Damasio, A. 2005. *Descartes' Error: Emotion, Reason, and the Human Brain.* New York: Penguin.

Davis, R., and C. J. Crompton. 2021. "What Do New Findings About Social Interaction in Autistic Adults Mean for Neurodevelopmental Research?" *Perspectives on Psychological Science* 16(3): 649–653.

Galvin, J., A. Howes, B. McCarthy, and G. Richards. 2021. "Self-Compassion as a Mediator of the Association Between Autistic Traits and Depressive/Anxious Symptomatology." *Autism* 25(2): 502–515.

Harmuth, E., E. Silletta, A. J. Bailey, and T. Adams. 2018. "Barriers and Facilitators to Employment for Adults with Autism: A Scoping Review." *Annals of International Occupational Therapy* 1(1): 31–40.

Harris, J. 2018. "Leo Kanner and Autism: A 75-Year Perspective." *International Review of Psychiatry* 30(1): 3–17.

Hendrickx, S. 2015. *Women and Girls with Autism Spectrum Disorder: Understanding Life Experiences from Early Childhood to Old Age.* London: Jessica Kingsley Publishers.

Jung, C. 2003. *Psychology and the Unconscious.* New York: Dover Publications.

Kenown, C. L. 2013. "Local Functional Overconnectivity in Posterior Brain Regions Is Associated with Symptom Severity in Autism Spectrum Disorders." *Cell Reports* 5: 567–572.

Khazan, O. 2020. "The Perks of Being a Weirdo: How Not Fitting in Can Lead to Creative Thinking." *The Atlantic,* April. https://www.theatlantic.com/magazine/archive/2020/04/the-perks-of-being-a-weirdo/606778.

Kinnaird, E., C. Stewart, and K. Tchanturia. 2019. "Investigating Alexithymia in Autism: A Systematic Review and Meta-Analysis." *European Psychiatry* 55: 80–89.

Kishmi, I., and F. Koga. 2018. *The Courage to Be Disliked.* New York: Atria Books.

Loos, H. G., and I. M. Loos Miller. 2004. "Shutdown States and Stress Instability in Autism." *Cuewave.*

Meilleur, A.-A. S., P. Jelenic, and L. Mottron. 2015. "Prevalence of Clinically and Empirically Defined Talents and Strengths in Autism." *Journal of Autism and Developmental Disorders* 45(5): 1354–1367.

Milton, D. E. M. 2012. "On the Ontological Status of Autism: The 'Double Empathy Problem.'" *Disability & Society* 27(6): 883–887.

Mitchell, A., and R. Pearce. 2021. "Prescribing Practice: An Overview of the Principles." *British Journal of Nursing* 30(17): 1016–1022.

Moss, P., W. Mandy, and P. Howlin. 2017. "Child and Adult Factors Related to Quality of Life in Adults with Autism." *Journal of Autism and Developmental Disorders* 47(6): 1830–1837.

Murray, D., M. Lesser, and W. Lawson. 2005. "Attention, Monotropism and the Diagnostic Criteria for Autism." *Autism* 9(2): 139–156.

Oakley, B. F. M., E. J. H. Jones, D. Crawley, T. Charman, J. Buitelaar, J. Tillmann, D. G. Murphy, E. Loth, and EU-AIMS LEAP Group. 2022. "Alexithymia in Autism: Cross-Sectional and Longitudinal Associations with Social-Communication Difficulties, Anxiety and Depression Symptoms." *Psychological Medicine* 52(8): 1458–1470.

Park, H. R., J. M. Lee, H. E. Moon, D. S. Lee, B.-N. Kim, J. Kim, D. G. Kim, and S. H. Paek. 2016. "A Short Review on the Current Understanding of Autism Spectrum Disorders." *Experimental Neurobiology* 25(1): 1–13.

Porges, S. 2017. *A Pocket Guide to Polyvagal Theory.* New York: W. W. Norton.

———. 2019. "Brain-Body Connection May Ease Autistic People's Social Problems." *Spectrum News*, August 20. https://www.spectrumnews.org/opinion/viewpoint/brain-body-connection -may-ease-autistic-peoples-social-problems.

Praslova, L. 2021. "Autism Doesn't Hold People Back at Work. Discrimination Does." *Harvard Business Review*, December 13. https://hbr.org/2021/12/autism-doesnt-hold-people-back-at -work-discrimination-does.

Prizant, B. 2022. *Uniquely Human: Updated and Expanded: A Different Way of Seeing Autism.* New York: Simon & Schuster.

Russo, F. 2018. "The Costs of Camouflaging Autism." *Spectrum News*, February 21. https:// www.spectrumnews.org/features/deep-dive/costs-camouflaging-autism.

Silberman, S. 2015. *NeuroTribes: The Legacy of Autism and the Future of Neurodiversity.* New York: Avery.

Uddin, L. Q. 2022. "Exceptional Abilities in Autism: Theories and Open Questions." *Current Directions in Psychological Science* 31(6): 509–517.

US Centers for Disease Control. 2022. "Autism Facts." https://www.cdc.gov/ncbddd/autism /facts.html.

US Department of Justice. 2023. "Introduction to the Americans with Disabilities Act." https://www.ada.gov/topics/intro-to-ada.

van Rooij, D., E. Anagnostou, C. Arango, G. Auzias, M. Behrmann, G. F. Busatto, et al. 2018. "Cortical and Subcortical Brain Morphometry Differences Between Patients with Autism Spectrum Disorder and Healthy Individuals Across the Lifespan: Results from the ENIGMA ASD Working Group." *American Journal of Psychiatry* 175(4): 359–369.

Wakefield, A. J., S. H. Murch, A. Anthony, J. Linnell, D. M. Casson, M. Malik, M. Berelowitz, et al. 1998. "RETRACTED: Ileal-Lymphoid-Nodular Hyperplasia, Non-Specific Colitis, and Pervasive Developmental Disorder in Children." *The Lancet* 351(9103): 609–686.

Warrier, V., and S. Baron-Cohen. 2017. "The Genetics of Autism." *Encyclopedia of Life Sciences.* http://lib.autismresearchcentre.com/papers/2017_Warrier_The-Genetics-of-Autism.pdf.

Welch, C., D. Cameron, M. Fitch, and H. Polatajko. 2020. "Living in Autistic Bodies: Bloggers Discuss Movement Control and Arousal Regulation." *Disability and Rehabilitation* 43(22): 3159–3167.

Wiskerke, J., H. Stern, and K. Igelström. 2018. "Camouflaging of Repetitive Movements in Autistic Female and Transgender Adults." *bioRxiv* 10. https://www.biorxiv.org/content/10 .1101/412619v1.

Jessica Penot, LPC-S, is a supervising licensed professional counselor in Madison, AL, who specializes in treating trauma and supporting autistic people. She has more than twenty years of clinical experience, is founder and director of Tree of Life Behavioral Health, and has spoken and written about autism on platforms, including *The Art of Autism* and *Psychology Today*. Penot was diagnosed autistic in her forties, and has spent a significant amount of time working to understand the specific challenges and traumas autistic women face. Her research and work focus primarily on issues involving the underdiagnosis and misdiagnosis of autistic women, and the impact it has on their lives and mental health. She is an advocate for neuro-affirmative approaches to treatment, and works to help facilitate autistic women in moving from being self-critical to self-compassionate. Her perspective on autism comes not only from her clinical experience, research, and study, but also from her lived experience.

Real change *is* possible

For more than forty-five years, New Harbinger has published proven-effective self-help books and pioneering workbooks to help readers of all ages and backgrounds improve mental health and well-being, and achieve lasting personal growth. In addition, our spirituality books offer profound guidance for deepening awareness and cultivating healing, self-discovery, and fulfillment.

Founded by psychologist Matthew McKay and Patrick Fanning, New Harbinger is proud to be an independent, employee-owned company. Our books reflect our core values of integrity, innovation, commitment, sustainability, compassion, and trust. Written by leaders in the field and recommended by therapists worldwide, New Harbinger books are practical, accessible, and provide real tools for real change.

 **new**harbinger**publications**

MORE BOOKS from
NEW HARBINGER PUBLICATIONS

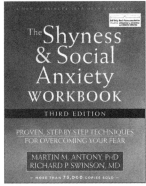
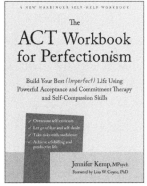

Did you know there are **free tools** you can download for this book?

Free tools are things like **worksheets**, **guided meditation exercises**, and **more** that will help you get the most out of your book.

You can download free tools for this book—whether you bought or borrowed it, in any format, from any source—from the New Harbinger website. All you need is a NewHarbinger.com account. Just use the URL provided in this book to view the free tools that are available for it. Then, click on the "download" button for the free tool you want, and follow the prompts that appear to log in to your NewHarbinger.com account and download the material.

You can also save the free tools for this book to your **Free Tools Library** so you can access them again anytime, just by logging in to your account! Just look for this button on the book's free tools page.

+ Save this to my free tools library

If you need help accessing or downloading free tools, visit **newharbinger.com/faq** or contact us at **customerservice@newharbinger.com.**